Purpose-Driven Learning

Purpose-Driven Learning advocates that the primary goal of education is to empower our students' innate drive to learn, which can be unlocked through the discovery and development of key social-emotional learning skills.

This book offers an intentional framework for exploring strategies of inclusion, social-emotional learning, and assessment that goes beyond abstract buzzwords. It features heartfelt stories, intriguing research, and effective action steps to inspire and empower teachers and their students to write authentic stories of social-emotional well-being and passionate, lifelong learning.

Purpose-Driven Learning is a process that can be explored and utilized in any educational context; teachers, coaches, camp directors, faith leaders, parents, and more will all find value in this resource.

Adam Moreno has explored social-emotional learning as a Drama teacher, theatre director, coach, pastor, and summer camp director. He is currently an educational consultant and has the honor of leading professional development presentations and workshops within a number of educational settings. Find out more at www.mrmoreno.com.

Purpose-Driven Learning

Unlocking and Empowering Our Students' Innate Passion for Learning

Adam Moreno

NEW YORK AND LONDON

Cover images: © Getty Images

First published 2023
by Routledge
605 Third Avenue, New York, NY 10158

and by Routledge
4 Park Square, Milton Park, Abingdon, Oxon, OX14 4RN

Routledge is an imprint of the Taylor & Francis Group, an informa business

© 2023 Taylor & Francis

The right of Adam Moreno to be identified as author of this work
has been asserted in accordance with sections 77 and 78 of the
Copyright, Designs and Patents Act 1988.

All rights reserved. No part of this book may be reprinted or
reproduced or utilised in any form or by any electronic, mechanical,
or other means, now known or hereafter invented, including
photocopying and recording, or in any information storage or
retrieval system, without permission in writing from the publishers.

Trademark notice: Product or corporate names may be trademarks
or registered trademarks, and are used only for identification and
explanation without intent to infringe.

Library of Congress Cataloging-in-Publication Data
Names: Moreno, Adam, author.
Title: Purpose-driven learning: unlocking and
empowering our students' innate passion for
learning / Adam Moreno.
Description: New York, NY: Routledge, 2022. |
Includes bibliographical references. |
Identifiers: LCCN 2021061772 (print) |
LCCN 2021061773 (ebook) | ISBN 9781032279152 (hardback) |
ISBN 9781032279138 (paperback) | ISBN 9781003294634 (ebook)
Subjects: LCSH: Affective education. | Motivation in education.
Classification: LCC LB1072 .M655 2022 (print) |
LCC LB1072 (ebook) | DDC 370.15/34–dc23/eng/20220124
LC record available at https://lccn.loc.gov/2021061772
LC ebook record available at https://lccn.loc.gov/2021061773

ISBN: 978-1-032-27915-2 (hbk)
ISBN: 978-1-032-27913-8 (pbk)
ISBN: 978-1-003-29463-4 (ebk)

DOI: 10.4324/9781003294634

Typeset in Palatino
by Newgen Publishing UK

To my students, my actors, my campers, and my youth group members:

Helping you write your own story of greatness has given my life true purpose.

Watching you share your greatness with the world has brought me overwhelming joy.

Contents

Foreword by Carolyn Karl ix
Acknowledgments xii

A Purpose-Driven Introduction 1

1 **Purpose-Driven Learning: Connecting, Exploring, Empowering** 10

2 **Intentional Belonging: Unconditional Inclusion and Affirmation** 25

3 **The Key of Confidence: The Journey of Becoming** 42

4 **The Key of Enthusiasm: Embracing a "Yes, I Can" Attitude** 59

5 **The Key of Focus: Looking Within, Raising Awareness Beyond** 74

6 **The Key of Initiative: Building Involvement and Increasing Impact** 90

7 **The Key of Creativity: Leveling Up with the Gamification Guru** 104

8 **The Key of Dependability: Showing Up and Doing Your Part** 118

9 **The Key of Curiosity: Exploring the Wonder Within Each Day** 132

viii ◆ Contents

10 **The Key of Empathy: Compassion, Curiosity, Connection**...148

11 **The Key of Resilience: Taking the Path Less Traveled** 164

12 **The Key of Effort: Being Better Than Before** 180

13 **Empowering Self-Assessment: Exploration and Expression** 194

Conclusion: A New Story of Learning.................208

Foreword

Some people come into your life and change you forever. Adam Moreno is the type of person remembered by almost everyone who crosses paths with him, even if just for a moment. He is driven, fearless, fun, and gifted at authentically connecting with others through stories.

My story with Adam began over ten years ago when he took the **initiative** to introduce himself to me following a church service. He enthusiastically volunteered to help with our middle and high school youth groups. As a church Youth Director and the mom of three kids who were part of the middle and high school youth groups, I was excited by the possibilities of what we could create together. It is always a challenge to find qualified people to help with ministry and here was an experienced leader who loved everything about working with youth. I felt like I had won the lottery!

I distinctly remember sitting on the hand-me-down couches in the youth room as Adam and I began planning activities and planting the seeds of our ministry partnership. Over a decade ago, Adam shared a framework he created for his Drama students – Purpose-Driven Learning. I was drawn to the ten key skills that help students unlock their passion for lifelong learning: Confidence, Enthusiasm, Focus, Initiative, Creativity, Dependability, Curiosity, Empathy, Resilience, and Effort. Over the years, it has become clear that these skills are also central themes in Adam's life as he seeks to live with purpose. As our friendship has grown and developed, this mindset of living with intentionality has become a central theme in my life, as well.

Confidence is one of the first qualities I noticed about Adam. He is confident in his abilities and is passionate about helping others build confidence in their abilities. I prefer to be a "behind the scenes" kind of leader, working hard but always putting the spotlight on others. Adam's confidence and support inspired me to intentionally challenge myself to be a public advocate. I challenged myself to move out of my comfort zone and strengthened my skills in the process.

Our partnership in ministry was fueled by our **enthusiasm** to provide a safe space for youth to be authentic in a community of belonging. Adam's **dependability** was exhibited by his willingness to attend weekly youth group meetings and chaperone our youth events. We utilized **creativity** while playing variations on tag – Adam and me against the youth. Adam would chase the youth, leading them in the direction we planned, while I, the less-athletic of the pair, would hide and tag everyone out as they ran past. Our creative approach worked every time, frustrating the most competitive youth, leaving them wondering how "the old folks" managed to win.

My family witnessed Adam's **focus** as he worked with his middle school students performing excellent plays and musicals, well beyond the caliber you would expect of non-professional children's theatre. Adam's creativity and **effort** led to the creation of Higher Expectations Theatre, where my daughter joined Adam as a high school student-director and intentionally explored her passion for theatre and teaching. After years of hearing about Red Arrow Camp, my kids and I decided to visit Adam at camp, exploring the beautiful surroundings. After a day taking in the sunshine and playing in the water, we watched the camp play, written and directed by Adam. Watching a hundred boys singing and dancing up on stage was a pretty spectacular sight. Adam consistently gives his best to all his endeavors and empowers those he works with to do the same.

Having worked together in youth ministry and knowing the central role faith plays in his life, I enthusiastically supported Adam as he explored his call to ordained ministry. Aware of the need for innovative Christian Education, Adam's **curiosity** led him to examine how he might connect his educational background more directly to his faith. As part of his seminary training, Adam worked as a pastoral intern at a congregation near where my family and I live. Our daughter had recently moved away for college, so we had an extra room available. Adam lived with us for a year, and Pastor Adam soon became "Uncle Adam."

An intentional focus on building **resilience** was a particular gift to me and my husband. Our lovingly described "knucklehead" twin boys were high school juniors at the time and were testing every boundary. Having another trusted adult in the house with a passion for learning from your mistakes and a mantra of "make good choices" was a gift to our family. Adam showed compassionate **empathy** for my twins' mischievous behavior, while routinely outsmarting them and holding them accountable.

It is clear that Adam is a teacher at heart – no matter the context or the title of his profession. Adam teaches by inspiring others and challenging those around him to be their best. Intentionally exploring Purpose-Driven Learning has helped me examine my own life. It has helped me move outside my comfort zone, develop and assess skills, and explore new opportunities. What started as an intentional change in my language led to a change in my perspective.

I am excited that years after first introducing this framework in his classroom and exploring it in his work with children, teens, and young adults, Adam has decided to write a book sharing his wisdom. But, readers, beware – it may forever change your perspective! It may drive you to challenge yourself in new ways and achieve things you could only ever imagine.

Carolyn Karl
Youth and Family Ministry
Program Director, Samaritan Family Wellness Foundation
Director of Faith Communities, REDgen
Friend for Life

Acknowledgments

There are so many people that I would like to thank, it is hard to know where to begin. As you may come to realize as you read this book, if it can be said in three words, I will say it in three paragraphs – so for the sake of brevity in at least one part of the book, I will seek to keep this short.

To God, my family, and my friends – your unconditional love and support have empowered me to confidently live an honest, authentic life. Thank you for affirming all of who I have been created to be.

To Michael, Carolyn, and Tim – you have challenged me to push myself, to grow, to learn, and to become more than I ever thought possible. The three of you were essential in my writing process and I could not have completed this book without you in my life. Thank you for your support.

To all of the children, teens, and young adults with whom I have journeyed on my many paths, you inspire me, you bring me happiness, and you offer my life meaning. Thank you for helping me create a story worth sharing with the world.

A Purpose-Driven Introduction

Purpose-Driven Learning

Driven to Learn

All great learning begins with the courage to ask bold questions – from the questions of early explorers driven to discover what lies beyond what is known to the questions of scientists throughout the ages driven to explore more deeply what we think is known, from the questions of mathematicians driven to seek the solutions to complex equations to the questions of artists driven to express the complex range of human emotions. As human beings, our questions drive our passions to explore, to grow, to discover, to create. It is a truth that stirs within all of us – our innate drive to learn.

Our students come with this drive already within them, already revealed in the questions they ask, already essential in how they express themselves, already informing how they engage the world. Schools must empower the discovery, explore the depths, and nurture the growth of this innate drive. Early in my teaching career, after years of working with children, teens, and young adults in a variety of settings, I was asked to intentionally reflect on a bold question that would dramatically change my teaching and my students' learning from that point further – *What is the purpose of school?*

A bold question? It seems like such a simple question, so simple that, too often, we forget to ask it, we assume we all agree,

DOI: 10.4324/9781003294634-1

and we believe that our students and their families are all on board. Yet disagreement about the purpose of school has fueled endless research, studies, discussions, arguments, conferences, teaching strategies, and educational pedagogies. And while I hope that you will continue reading this whole book, which is, more or less, my answer to this question, I am completely aware of the countless educational books out there trying to answer the same question with a diversity of perspectives, different conclusions, and varying degrees of success.

So take a moment and consider your response – what is the purpose of school? Is it to help our children learn to read and write, understand how the world works, know the facts about what has come before, or be able to offer the right answer when presented with a problem? Is the purpose of school to help our students to get good grades to validate their learning, to get into the best colleges to continue their learning, or to score high on their ACTs or SATs to demonstrate their learning? Can we intentionally clarify and offer strategic action around buzzwords like "rigor," "excellence," and "success?" Making the question more personal – what is the purpose of your classroom? Can we demand more from our students than successfully regurgitating content, more from our teaching than simply rewarding trained compliance, and more from our administration than merely providing hoops to jump through in order to "prove" required learning? In my career as a teacher and in my work with teachers of many grade levels in a variety of content areas, I know most educators agree that the purpose of school, the purpose of their classrooms needs to be more than what our current educational system mandates.

What would your reaction be if I claimed that the purpose of school should not focus on content knowledge, cannot be demonstrated through standardized tests, and is not reflected in grades? Would you put down this book and stop reading because you disagree with the idea of demanding more from our educational system? Perhaps it's not that you disagree, but rather you believe that our educational system is so entrenched in content, testing, and grades that books on challenging and changing the system should be on the shelf with other "fictional" writings. What do you believe – nothing needs to be done or nothing can be done? Or, like me, do you embrace a belief that, in defining our purpose and teaching with intentionality, we can impact an entire system one school, one classroom, one student at a time? Here is my bold claim:

> The purpose of school is to unlock and empower the drive for authentic, holistic lifelong learning that is innate in every person.

This is not some newfangled teaching and learning pedagogical trend. This purpose challenges us to return to a fundamental truth of humanity that we all know and all have experienced: A passion for learning *is* innate. Therefore, formal education must serve to help students explore this innate drive, discover the key skills needed to unlock their potential for growth, and empower our students to embrace this passion for learning during their time with us and beyond their time in school. Whether you agree or disagree with this purpose, I invite you to explore Purpose-Driven Learning (PDL) with a beginner's mindset: wonder instead of judgment, curiosity instead of criticism, and imagination instead of resistance – enthusiastic exploration, sincere openness, and creative engagement.

More Than a Program – a Pedagogy

Creating PDL, a pedagogy rooted in intentionality, required me to unlearn poor "traditional" educational practices and explore dynamic, new strategies. I needed to look with a constructive and critical eye at everything I was taught as an educator – my teaching style and methodology, my curricular design and lesson plans, my approach to discipline and classroom management techniques, and my homework policies and assessment strategies.

"Unlearning" requires an open and resilient mindset and I needed to honestly reflect on my own learning, my strengths and limitations, my purpose and passion. How did I learn in school and how do I learn now? What motivates me to set goals, learn new things, and take risks? Why did I become a teacher and what do I hope to offer my students? In reflecting on and answering these questions, it became clear that how I was teaching was not aligned with how I enjoy learning, how I feel inspired, or how I pursue my passions. A sincere desire to help my students confront the challenges of performing in Drama class led me to spoon-feed expectations, offer false praise, accept ridiculous excuses, kowtow to parent demands, and use grades as incentives. On the other side of the coin, my fears around Drama class not being taken seriously or being a "fluff" class led me to implement ineffective practices that required, enforced, and disciplined – trying to control all that I thought was within my power to control.

Along with self-reflection of my efforts to unlearn and relearn, I knew that I needed to listen to my students about their process of learning and observe their responses to my teaching. I discovered that there was a lot of anxiety around getting an "A," a lot of doubt around their abilities to perform, and a lot of fear around failing – especially on stage in front of their peers. Anxiety led my students, in my early years of teaching, to simply do exactly what the rubric told them to do to get a good grade – no real creativity, solution-seeking, or original demonstrations of their learning. Their doubt led some of them to give up before even trying, because they "knew they weren't good at Drama." And their fears led to them trying to avoid the risk of performing, making excuses of being "shy," and claiming to not like my class because it was "dumb."

Don't get me wrong, the majority of my students did the work expected of them in my class and "liked" me as a teacher – but I knew that doing the work and liking me were not purposes for my classroom that would lead to impactful learning or lasting development. I knew that something had to intentionally change so that the effort put forth was their best and was self-motivated. I needed to intentionally tap into their love of exploring, of challenging themselves, of growing, and of learning that I knew was there.

A Space of Belonging

As I sought to intentionally shift the focus of my teaching and the purpose of my students' learning, I knew that I needed to create a space in which they felt safe, affirmed, celebrated, and empowered. I hear a lot of talk about the need for students to explore, take risks, and confront their fears. The majority of this book emphasizes the need to intentionally focus on our students' social-emotional well-being – yet, before we can encourage these high expectations and promote the vulnerability needed for social-emotional learning (SEL) exploration, teachers must take on the challenging work of creating a learning space of belonging. This book begins with the same reflection each of us must take as we begin to transform our classrooms – how do we holistically and unconditionally affirm every student in our classroom? Students who do not feel included and affirmed will struggle with the internal confidence needed to boldly share with others their authentic selves. If we have students ashamed of their authenticity or afraid of having this authentic self rejected, how can they experience belonging? And if they do not experience belonging, they will never be empowered to fully discover and develop their innate greatness.

An Intentional Language of Learning

In order for us to learn and grow together, we must establish a common language of learning. Without such language, there is confusion, misunderstanding, and, at times, frustration and apathy. With my students, we discuss what I mean when I talk about them being successful. *Success* is not "winning," nor is it being perfect. Success is not simply a standard measured at the completion of a performance or the end of the school year. Success is not a destination. Success, as understood in my Drama program, is measured throughout the learning process, it is rooted in articulating our SEL, and it is self-assessed with feedback from one another.

The same clarity is needed with all of our educational buzzwords. I am not saying they are "bad" – in fact, I use quite a number of buzzwords throughout this book. However, my goal is to make sure I explain how I understand each word, how I intentionally use them in my classroom, and how my students are empowered to articulate these words into the development and demonstration of their learning. *Holistic well-being* and *authentic, lifelong learning* sound great on classroom posters, in emails to parents, and, not gonna lie, on a cover of a book. However, without intentional exploration and explanation, they, unfortunately, run the risk of losing their powerful meaning. As I share PDL with you, I want you to know that I have experienced how it can have an impact on the whole child, in and out of school, at all ages. It impacts individual efforts and collaborative endeavors, when they are struggling and when they are thriving. It is rooted in self-discovery, self-development, and self-assessment because the journey of learning must begin with one's own innate drive in order to have a transformative impact – holistic well-being and authentic, lifelong learning.

So let's be intentional with our language – what do schools mean who claim educational *rigor* – the definition of the word is strictness, severity, or harshness; an inflexibility in opinion. YIKES – that is a pillar of learning in your school? Or how about *Excellence in Education* – first, who isn't striving for excellence? I have never encountered a school striving for mediocrity – I mean, plenty of schools are achieving standard mediocrity, but I have never seen it celebrated on a banner. So, if we claim excellence, what does it mean? In my Drama program, we talk a lot about *achieving greatness*. It is not something judged by others. Greatness is an internal awareness of achievement. It is about intentionally setting out in the morning to be the best version of yourself you can, about seeking out learning and growth, about admitting stumbles and falls along the way, about connecting with and helping out others, and at the end of the day, it is about being able to confidently point to ways that the world was a better place because you were in it that day. We are *all* capable of greatness!

The majority of chapters in this book explore the Keys of Purpose-Driven Learning – the ten SEL skills which unlock and empower our passion for learning: Confidence, Enthusiasm, Focus, Creativity, Initiative, Dependability, Curiosity, Empathy, Resilience, Effort. The Keys of PDL are the intentional language of learning I have used throughout my work with children, teens, and young adults – and with adults (but don't tell the parents of my students and my congregation members that I used my classroom strategy on them). These skills align with the five core SEL competencies defined by the Collaborative for Academic, Social, and Emotional Learning, which we'll explore in more depth in the chapter on Empowering Self-Assessment (CASEL, 2020).

As we dive into the ten Keys of PDL, let me assure you that these words work. Once taught to the students, the Keys of PDL truly become language that they use to assess and articulate their learning. It is really quite remarkable to experience a sixteen-year-old express remorse for not being a dependable member of a group project or express pride in taking the initiative to come in for extra help before a test. I have had a seven-year-old reflect on the resilience needed to overcome the "obstacle" of eating his green beans during dinner at camp and have listened to an eleven-year-old articulate the empathy she sought to express during our mission trip with church. Children, teens, and young adults will embrace and use this language of learning when it is consistent and intentional.

Yet the Keys of PDL are not written in stone. They don't hold special magical power – they are tested, they have proven to hold meaning and have an impact, and they are a way for you and your students to be intentional with your SEL language. However, if a key seems to be ineffective in your context, explore other language. Teach your students the synonyms found on the posters or discovered in their own exploration and have them connect their language back to the Keys of PDL. A shared language for learning is essential and the intentional implementation of this language is important. So give it a fair try, approach it with openness – and as you apply it within your classroom and explore it with your students, be flexible to tweaks, adaptations, and changes needed for your context. Being Purpose-Driven is *not* about us all being the same. Being Purpose-Driven is about us all intentionally unlocking and empowering our students' passion for learning. Let me offer you some key language, but at the end of the day, use whatever keys free your students to boldly

Mindful Reflection

We can tell our students that they are great. We can tell them that they need to improve, focus on specific development, praise certain skills, and hold them accountable for words and actions. However, if all of the learning and growth assessed within our classrooms comes from us, it will be insufficient and incomplete. Our feedback to students is an important aspect of our guidance of their learning journey, but our feedback must be rooted in their own self-assessment. In an affirming space of belonging, empowered with a language of learning explored within the Keys of PDL, our students can reflect on, internalize, and articulate their own perspective of their social-emotional health and well-being, their struggles in learning, and their confidence in specific skills. At the end of this book, we will explore the power of self-assessment within our classrooms. Developing our students' ability to effectively self-assess requires intentionality and regularity. In little ways, every day, and in meaningful ways at key points throughout the school year, we must allow our students to stop, breathe, reflect, and assess how far they have come, where they are at, and how they can continue to move forward in their learning journey.

Change in Focus

Now, this is not one of those "alarmist" books that claim everything that we are doing is horrifically wrong and that if we don't change by using the strategies in this book our precious children are doomed. In fact, I believe we can start off by giving ourselves a pat on the back, a little round of applause, because the truth is, effective teachers care and connect with students. I know that we all sincerely try to address the needs of the whole child and, more often than not, do more than simply develop our students academically. Effective teachers develop SEL skills within their students, even if or when they are not aware of it. If you are truly exploring PDL to discover ways to strengthen your teaching, to empower your students, and to transform your classroom, you are far more than "just an effective teacher," you are a driven educator. Through this book, I hope to inspire and empower you to do what you are doing, be the great teacher you already are – just with more intentionality focused on the importance of inspiring and empowering our students' innate passion for learning. So let's begin our Purpose-Driven journey – we'll share stories, examine our teaching, explore new possibilities, and encourage intentional steps forward as we seek to have a meaningful impact on our students so that they can be the authors of their own stories of learning – stories of true belonging, social-emotional health, and mindful reflection.

Reference

CASEL. (2020). *SEL: What Are the Core Competence Areas and Where Are They Promoted?*. Retrieved 4 March 2021, from https://casel.org/sel-framework/.

1

Purpose-Driven Learning: Connecting, Exploring, Empowering

Connecting to My Story

The Power of Storytelling

I want to build a relationship with you. I want you to know who I am. I want you to connect with my experiences. I want you to trust that what I am sharing with you is true and transformative! We know that relationships can be established in all kinds of ways. Back in the day, pen-pals formed connections through handwritten letters; more recently, technology allows us to connect through email, text, and social media. Those of us teaching in 2020 needed to build relationships with our students through distance learning – more challenging than in-person learning, but I know that we were able to achieve a connection with our students that made an impact. While lasting relationships might be more difficult when not created face-to-face, they are not impossible – so let's venture into the challenge. Let's connect, reflect, learn, and grow together.

It is my hope that this book will help empower us in this challenge. Each of these chapters will begin with a story because it is through our stories that we reveal who we are. Stories allow

DOI: 10.4324/9781003294634-2

us to share our experiences that make us similar, and through our stories we can affirm the differences within our experiences that make us unique. Research shows that when you "listen to a story, your brain waves actually start to synchronize with those of the storyteller. And reading a narrative activates brain regions involved in deciphering or imagining a person's motives and perspective" (Renken, 2020). In other words, we can empathetically connect through storytelling and begin to develop an authentic relationship.

My stories come from the diverse roles I have had in working with children, teens, and young adults. I share stories of my students, campers, and youth, as well as stories from my own childhood about my teachers, my coaches, my mentors, and even a couple of stories about my family. If learning is limitless, then why limit my stories to the Purpose-Driven Learning (PDL) that occurs in my classroom? However, it's not just about my stories. I also listen carefully to my students' stories – stories of their families, of their hobbies, of their frustrations, and of their dreams. I listen (sometimes I jot down a few discreet notes) and I bring up what they talked about at a later date. If you want to build a meaningful relationship with students, ask how their "big game" went next time you see them, check in to see how their dog is doing after they tell you she is sick, joke around about their latest "fight" with their sibling, have them tell you about the drawings they were working on in your study hall – listen to their stories, actively respond, and find ways to revisit their stories to demonstrate true care and interest.

So let's build a relationship – *let me tell you a story*. I begin by sharing with you three of my passions: summer camps, theatre, and my faith. These passions led to my three most meaningful careers as a camp director, a Drama teacher, and a youth pastor. Yeah, pretty fun jobs that required *a lot* of energy and enthusiasm, but centered around my greatest passion – connecting to and impacting the lives of children, teens, and young adults! I hope that my stories throughout this book will help us begin to form a lasting relationship in which we can share more stories about the transformation within our classrooms, beyond our schools, and equally as important, the transformation deep within ourselves.

A Summer Like No Other

Did you go to a camp when you were a child or teen? Perhaps, like me, you went to several – a couple of week-long sports camps, super-cool band camp, a two-week church camp, even a YMCA day camp every now and then. I liked camp growing up, and after my junior year of high school, I was hired to work in the kitchen and be the wrestling instructor at Red Arrow Camp (RAC) for boys, a seven-week residential, sports, and wilderness camp in the Northwoods of Wisconsin. It was life-changing! I worked over the summer at RAC since 1998, as a counselor and coach, then as leadership staff, and now I have spent a number of years on their advisory board. Some of my best friends are my Red Arrow brothers, for whom I am extremely thankful. Yet it was for two other reasons that RAC changed my life.

It was at Red Arrow that I was introduced to the great outdoors and it instilled in me a passion for hiking, canoeing, cycling, and running (for fun). I love being outside, especially when it involves physical activity, grand adventures, and exploring the wonders of the wilderness. It was at Red Arrow, I also discovered my passion for working with kids. Up to that point, I had never been in charge of, been a mentor for, or been responsible for children. I loved helping the boys learn new skills, face their fears, overcome challenges, work together with their cabinmates, and reflect on being their best selves. We have a saying at Red Arrow: "Don't wait to be a great man, be a great boy." I didn't call the work I did as a counselor "Purpose-Driven Learning," nor in those early years did I use the language of social-emotional learning (SEL) to describe the campers' growth at camp – but I knew camp was powerful and I knew that I was empowering my campers to be "great boys" by building essential lifelong skills. After four summers at RAC, I decided to change majors and become a teacher – an all-too-common story for camp counselors. It was at Red Arrow where I discovered my love for teaching.

All the World's a Stage

The people who have only known me as an adult are often surprised when they find out that I did not grow up as a theatre kid. My passion for theatre is such a defining aspect of who I am. It is hard to believe that my theatrical journey began by participating in only two high school musicals. It is true – two chorus roles in high school inspired me to pursue a musical theatre degree. From college, I headed out to the East Coast to try my hand at professional theatre. After four years out East, I had the opportunity to return back to my hometown of Milwaukee to teach middle school theatre at a top independent K12 school. It was a tough decision to give up one dream to pursue another – but the opportunity to help young people reach their theatrical dreams motivated the change.

So I returned to Milwaukee and summers at RAC, and began my career as the Drama teacher and theatre director – and my life has never been the same. It was during these years that I truly experienced the transformative power of the arts in the lives of young people, as strong administrative support of the arts met the passionate gifts of Arts educators and the innate creativity of children. I was granted the freedom to create innovative curriculum, implement creative teaching strategies, and explore diverse methods for empowering students in their own learning. Being the theatre director and choreographer made it possible for me to express my artistic vision and empower my students to boldly explore and express theirs. My experience teaching allowed me to start my own children's theatre company, Higher Expectations Theatre, where I worked with elementary through high school-aged students, unlocking and empowering life skills through theatre skills.

As I have pursued my passion for theatre education, I have gathered experiences and gained expertise that now offer me the opportunity to be a national speaker promoting PDL. I am honored to have the opportunity to lead workshops in building essential SEL skills through arts integration at educational conferences and professional development trainings all over the country. Fast forward from a sixteen-year-old, with an undiscovered passion for theatre, to my life now, in which theatre has become foundational to who I am, how I express myself, and how I engage the world around me.

Can I Get an Amen

My faith has always been an important aspect of who I am. I grew up going to a faith-based school, went to church, and in my adult life have volunteered as a Sunday School teacher, Confirmation mentor, and youth leader. For almost a decade, I taught in a formal classroom and directed on the school stage. I passionately pursued my vocation as an Arts educator and I taught with the intention to inspire and empower the skills of PDL in my students. Yet, on the weekends, I sought to help inspire and empower the faith of children and young adults in my faith community.

In 2015, out of the blue, I was "distracted" by curiosity! I looked up from my passion for theatre education to look a little closer at something else – faith-based education. Then I started thinking: "What if?" What if I take the innovative teaching strategies I learned as a Drama teacher and apply them in ministry? What if I take the educational technologies I used in my classroom and use them in a church setting? What if PDL can help others be more intentional in their faith? And just like that, curiosity changed my life. Well, actually it took a lot of discernment and prayer, but I felt called to follow my curiosity into a new vocation. Like a hummingbird, as Elizabeth Gilbert might suggest, I moved from one beautiful field of flowers to another, bringing some of the old to the new, "cross-pollinating" in hopes of creating something more beautiful.

After three years of seminary, I was ordained as a pastor within the Evangelical Lutheran Church in America (ELCA), a progressive and affirming body of Christian believers. It was in my time within a congregation working with all ages in faith-based education that I realized how impactful SEL skills are beyond the classroom. More than simply developing key SEL skills, it was during my time in ministry that I came to know the transformative power of belonging in the process of becoming one's best self. Within the context of my ELCA congregations, I proclaimed and experienced the power of radical inclusion and compassionate affirmation of every person.

If it was at Red Arrow that I discovered my passion for teaching, then it was through my faith journey that I experienced what kind of educator I actively sought to be each and every day – open and affirming to the vast diversity of individuals with whom I would engage, helping all to discover their created identity and develop the innate greatness that lies inside of each of them.

Holistic Education

As I stepped away from congregational ministry, the opportunity to write a book became available to me. A number of my educational Twitter colleagues had written books, and while I was pursuing ministry, they had done the hard yet rewarding work of becoming authors, national conference speakers, and highly sought-after professional development presenters. My former colleague and best friend, Michael Matera, suggested that I write a book – after all, PDL has been so impactful in his gamified classroom that he wrote about it in his book *Explore Like A Pirate* (Matera, 2015). If unlocking and empowering SEL worked for me and worked for him (and many of those who read his book), why not write my own book? So I did.

However, it would be foolish of me to write only about my experience in a formal educational setting – especially about a Purpose-Driven process that claims to unlock and empower authentic, holistic lifelong learning. I am an educator – in the classroom, on the theatre stage, at camp, and within my faith communities. We are all educators beyond our classrooms – within our families, as part of diverse communities, and throughout the world, as we connect and collaborate with others over social media and virtual educational platforms. From stories of summer camp to youth group, from stories of my Drama classroom to the various classrooms in which I have been a substitute teacher, the power of PDL is continually affirmed and continually surprises me as it unlocks and empowers the innate passion for learning within young people in such dynamic ways. It may seem impossible and yet the stories shared in each chapter are true – trust me, give PDL a try, and begin to create your own unbelievable stories within your classroom and beyond.

Reflecting on Your Story

We All Have a Story

My experiences, my stories, are just that – mine. While I hope that there are moments with which you can connect, there will certainly be moments that vary greatly from your experiences, from your story. In the following chapters, after I share my stories, I will give you the opportunities to reflect on your story. Where do you feel connection? Where do you experience resistance? What are your thoughts on the stories that I share, on the Key of PDL being explored? I hope that the questions I ask in each chapter help you pause from reading my words and consider your own thoughts and feelings.

An essential step in teaching, building, and empowering social-emotional skills is being open to exploring these skills within ourselves. You don't have to be an expert in, nor do you have to be strong at, every SEL skill. In fact, that would be impossible. Rather, each of us needs to reflect on our strengths and challenges, just as we are going to ask our students to do. We need to embrace our strengths with humility, yet with confidence. We need to admit our limitations without shame and with a growth mindset – knowing that we can learn and grow in any skills we commit to exploring. You are the author of your story and I know you'll write a story that is truly amazing! So:

- ♦ What is your story so far in your career, in your life? Passions? Failures? Successes?
- ♦ What experiences have shaped your story? Childhood? Family? Career? Interests?
- ♦ What is the story you wish to write as you journey forward? Goals? Purpose? Dreams?
- ♦ What is your WHY? WHY did you start teaching? WHY do you feel it is an important and/or needed career? WHY do you show up each and every day?

Exploring Our "WHY"

Where Do We Start?

Years ago, I read Simon Sinek's book *Start With Why*, and its overall message and his challenge to his readers have stuck with me long after reading. "For those who have an open mind for new ideas, who seek to create long-lasting success, and who believe that your success requires the aid of others, I offer you a challenge. From now on, start with WHY" (Sinek, 2011). The book shares stories of successful individuals and organizations, it provides research based on inspiration, motivation, and innovation, and its companion "workbook," *Find Your Why* (Sinek, 2017), offers practical exercises and applications for defining one's purpose and embracing the power of intentionality.

Fully believing in the power of WHY, my book explores the purpose of school – asking WHY SCHOOL? Why do we require children from six to eighteen years old to spend almost eight hours, five days a week in our school building, in our classrooms? Why are the subjects we teach important? Why do we choose to teach this content over that content? Why grade students' learning and why must everyone demonstrate their learning in standardized ways? WHY? It is a powerful question.

It wouldn't be fair to ask "why" of our current educational system without asking why of the pedagogy I am promoting. Why Purpose-Driven Learning? Why must we change the purpose of our classrooms? Why do I believe that the answer to a passion for lifelong learning lies within intentionally discovering, developing, and demonstrating a diversity of SEL skills? WHY?

The beginning of each chapter builds our relationship through stories so that our learning is grounded in trust – a trust in the importance of the SEL skills being explored. Yet our learning need not simply be anecdotal. Moving from our stories into a deeper exploration of our WHY allows us to build upon trust and validates experiential learning with research and data. Why do you need to explore PDL – well, it worked for me, as revealed in my stories, but perhaps that is not enough of a reason for you, or maybe it's not enough for your students, parents, or your administrators? Then let's explore our WHY by exploring the books of other educators and experts in the field, the studies of universities, and the research of educational institutions. There is so much data out there and it overwhelmingly supports a focus on SEL.

This section of each chapter is not going to be some dry, complicated, academic argument for the need for SEL in education. Rather, I have tried to keep the research accessible and relatable. If you would like to explore the books, studies, and research referenced in the chapter more deeply, I invite you to check out the bibliography at the end of each chapter. PDL works and makes a huge impact in the lives of those I teach and mentor. Trust me or trust the research – or even better, trust both!

Social-Emotional Learning

There are so many educational topics to explore, to learn about, to try in our classrooms, so why focus on the development of our students' social-emotional intelligence (SEI)? Let me state why in no uncertain terms – SEI is the foundation of all learning, growth, and relationships. Developing our ability to reflect on our feelings, affirm our emotions, and adapt the expression of these emotions all require strong SEI. Setting a course of action, working toward achieving our goals, and assessing (perhaps reassessing) our plan to keep moving forward all require strong SEI. Articulating our thoughts to others, listening to others' perspectives with open minds, and using new information to change our understanding all require strong SEI. Collaborating with others, disagreeing constructively, and negotiating compromise all require strong SEI – and strong SEI is unlocked and empowered when SEL is the foundation of the authentic relationships we build with our students, the focus of our teaching within and beyond the classroom, and the framework of our holistic assessment of our students' growth.

The Collaborative for Academic, Social, and Emotional Learning (CASEL) understand that SEL is "an integral part of education and human development" and define it as

Purpose-Driven Learning ◆ 19

the process through which all young people and adults acquire and apply the knowledge, skills, and attitudes to develop healthy identities, manage emotions and achieve personal and collective goals, feel and show empathy for others, establish and maintain supportive relationships, and make responsible and caring decisions.

(CASEL, 2020)

In other words, SEL is the process through which our students discover, develop, and demonstrate their SEI.

Reflecting on my careers, I am aware that everything connects back to SEI. When there was a rainy day at camp – I needed to tap into my creativity and come up with something fun for eight nine-year-old boys. When I had a disagreement with the tech director on the scene design – I needed to actively listen to her ideas and constructively reach a decision that honored her role and expertise. In preaching every single Sunday – I needed to take the initiative to look up new perspectives on the same "old" Bible verses and put forth the effort throughout the week to prepare a meaningful message.

If everything connects back to SEI for me, I can be confident that it all connects back to SEI for my campers, students, and youth. Why focus on SEL – because my campers will need resilience to overcome homesickness. Why SEL – because my students will need to tap into their curiosity to explore challenging Shakespearean language. Why SEL – because the youth in my congregation will need to demonstrate that they are dependable members of the faith community, willing to contribute, even when their parents are not "making them." Why SEL – because in every aspect of their lives, the young people I work with will need a strong awareness of and confidence in their SEI that they have intentionally discovered, developed, and demonstrated within my Purpose-Driven cabin, classroom, and congregation.

Inspiring Our Students' Stories

This book has my stories and it has the stories of authors and researchers who are experts in the field of SEL. You bring your stories as you read and reflect – your lived experiences that have made you who you are, influenced how you express yourself, and impacted how you connect with others and the world around you. Yet, even as much as I love the spotlight, learning is not all about me, it is not all about the research, nor is it all about you. Yes, our stories are essential, but we must emphasize, explore, and engage the stories of our students. After my stories, after reflecting on your story, after exploring why, each chapter will invite you to consider how the Key of PDL that is being explored connects to your students' stories.

I am not you. Your students are not my students. While I believe that SEL skills are essential in the learning and growth of *all* people, how we talk about these skills, how we implement these skills, and how we assess these skills might be different. Culturally affirming SEL exploration requires us to embrace our different contexts and communities, deeply reflect on who our students are, what they need, and how we connect with them through meaningful relationships. In reflecting on "the current narrative around SEL," Education Anew Fellow Cierra Kaler-Jones writes,

> True SEL is about understanding our relationships with ourselves and with others. It's to know ourselves as holistic human beings, and to be able to see the humanity in others to fight, together, for the world we deserve, which is rooted in equity and justice.
>
> (Kaler-Jones, 2020)

How I challenged my middle school students at a suburban, independent school *is* different from how an elementary school teacher might challenge his second-grade students within an urban charter school, which will be different from how an AP Chemistry teacher will challenge her students at a rural public school. Age, content area, the surrounding community, cultural awareness, parental involvement, and administrative support all play a role in how we live into and live out our purpose of unlocking and empowering our students' passion for learning. Yet, no matter our context, our SEL exploration and expression must address both our individual well-being and the connection to our shared humanity with all people.

I write from my perspective, about my experiences. I have tried to reflect on my biases and blindspots. I have tried to share stories with which most of you can connect. I have sought to provide research from a diversity of authors and experts, and I seek to offer strategies that can be adapted and used in any classroom – but even with this intentionality, there will be holes, miscommunications, and missed opportunities. Please, take the time to reflect on the questions about your context offered in each chapter. You know your students. Perhaps ask your students these questions and take time to listen to their responses – their answers may surprise you. This section in each chapter can be a start to meaningful conversations about these Keys of PDL and will go a long way in establishing the relationships needed for truly collaborative teaching and learning.

- ♦ How is your story different from your students' stories? In what ways are they similar?
- ♦ What SEL skills might your students embrace? Which skills might they be resistant to discovering and developing?
- ♦ Can your students' parents and/or families support your efforts in exploring SEL skills with their children?
- ♦ What will be the benefits of intentionally exploring PDL with your students? What may be the challenges? How can you be proactive in addressing these challenges?

Unlocking and Empowering Purpose-Driven Learning

Something More

Stories can inspire. Research can validate. Yet, for this book to be truly empowering, I strongly feel that it needs to offer practical advice and action steps. Too often, SEL "programs" are nothing more than banners and posters with overused quotes, clichéd catchphrases, and abstract buzzwords. For PDL to be truly impactful, it must be practical. Don't get me wrong – there are posters, but it is my hope that the posters are a resource that leads to action. However, action with abstract character skills can be challenging. We may be able to understand *why* focusing on SEL skills is important, but many of us struggle to effectively and intentionally put into regular practice *how* to motivate, develop, and assess these skills. Each chapter will end with practical takeaways – language to use, techniques to implement, strategies to explore. I have used them in my classroom and in my work with young people outside of a formal school setting and they work. Give them a try, adapt them as you see fit for your context, toss out what doesn't work, and keep what unlocks and empowers growth and greatness!

You Gotta Believe

The biggest challenge I face when offering professional development for other educators is the claim that "their students would never do these activities" – or worse, that their students "can't" do these suggestions. There is no other claim that gets me more riled up, either. Of course, your students *can* do these things – your students *can* do anything. You have to believe in them, no matter how many times they may challenge your belief. Set and maintain high expectations around SEL and hold your students to them. Show them that failing to meet the expectations isn't the end of the world, remind them that we all fail, and help them give it another go (which is actually still developing SEL skills). Don't let them settle for "good enough" and celebrate with them when SEL accomplishments are achieved. *All* children are capable of great things! Don't count them out, don't discredit their drive, don't limit them without even giving them the opportunity to demonstrate to you that they *can* and they *will*.

Invest the Time

With your guidance and support, your students can build a learning environment in which all can thrive. Yet taking the risk of exploring that which is innate, that which is undiscovered, that which is within requires a safe and supportive community in which to open up, explore, and share one's authentic self with others. This is not achieved in a singular "team-building" activity or trust exercise. It is accomplished through a commitment of time and energy at the beginning of the year or semester to building relationships. It is grown in daily reminders, in every class throughout the school year, of expectations regarding inclusion, accountability when words or actions are at odds with these expectations, and regular opportunities to develop and demonstrate these expectations. A safe and supportive learning environment actively invites and intentionally welcomes all to participate in the collaborative process of learning.

Assessing the Abstract

Once we have explored all ten Keys of PDL, we need to take intentional time to address the assessment of SEL. Notice I say "the assessment of" and not "the grading of" SEL skills. Can a student really get an "A" in confidence or a "4" in empathy? How do you grade resilience – give them an "F" and see how they overcome "failure?" The final chapter of this book looks at the challenges of assessing somewhat abstract characteristics and offers my thoughts and techniques for communicating meaningful feedback. Throughout the book, we will discuss strategies for making these SEL skills less abstract; however, that doesn't mean the concrete methods and activities should be graded. Through effective self-assessment and constructive teacher feedback, we can offer students, their parents, and our administration impactful information about the SEI of each student in our classroom. And spoiler: It doesn't require endless hours of comment writing for the teacher!

A Transformative Approach

PDL is not a "one-and-done" program. It is more than just the dynamic kick-off to your school, more than an activity done in your advising homeroom, more than a mid-year grade-level assembly, and more than just a bunch of words to throw into the comment section of your students' report cards at the end of the year. PDL can have a meaningful impact in your individual classroom for you and your students, but let the power of intentionality cast a wider net. When a Purpose-Driven approach is coordinated with your colleagues, supported by the families of your students, initiated by your administration, or empowered throughout your whole district, it becomes even stronger. PDL is relational and it is communal – the greater the involvement of everyone within one's community, the greater the impact.

So let me tell you a powerful story of PDL – unlocked through everyday opportunities, found in ordinary moments, discovered in the unexpected, and revealed through dynamic and diverse connections. It is a story that empowers bold exploration and authentic relationships. It is rooted in the strong foundation of SEL and celebrated within supportive communities! Welcome to the PDL community! You are invited to become part of this remarkable story. I am confident that together we are going to inspire the stories of our students that will impact the world.

References

CASEL. (2020). *What Is SEL?*. Retrieved 28 March 2021, from https://casel.org/what-is-sel/.

Kaler-Jones, C. (2020). *When SEL Is Used as Another Form of Policing*. Retrieved 28 March 2021, from https://medium.com/@justschools/when-sel-is-used-as-another-form-of-policing-fa53cf85dce4.

Matera, M. (2015). *Explore Like a Pirate: Gamification and Game-Inspired Course Design to Engage, Enrich, and Elevate Your Learners*. San Diego: Dave Burgess Consulting, Inc.

Renken, E. (2020). *How Stories Connect and Persuade Us: Unleashing the Brain Power of Narrative*. Retrieved 10 August 2020, from www.npr.org/sections/health-shots/2020/04/11/815573198/how-stories-connect-and-persuade-us-unleashing-the-brain-power-of-narrative.

Sinek, S. (2017). *Find Your Why: A Practical Guide for Discovering Purpose for You and Your Team*. London: Portfolio Penguin.

Sinek, S. (2011). *Start with Why: How Great Leaders Inspire Everyone to Take Action*. London: Portfolio Penguin.

2

Intentional Belonging: Unconditional Inclusion and Affirmation

Connecting to My Story

A Controversial Topic

Those who know me know that I do not shy away from challenging conversations and difficult discussions. In fact, I rather enjoy offering contrary perspectives, addressing the elephant in the room, or bringing up the "taboo" topics of politics and religion in "polite" company. It should come as no surprise, then, that after the general overview of Purpose-Driven Learning (PDL) offered in the opening chapter, I jump right into a chapter filled with controversy – the need for teachers to create a space of belonging within their classroom. You might be thinking: How can belonging be controversial? Doesn't every teacher strive to have a "safe and supportive" learning environment? The short answer is no – no, there are many teachers who do not prioritize belonging and do not believe that it is their responsibility to address the social-emotional needs of their students. Teach the content, prepare students for the next grade level, and ensure they perform well on the standardized tests that determine funding – that is the "job" for many teachers. The long

DOI: 10.4324/9781003294634-3

answer – well, we have an entire chapter to delve into the long answer, but as the chapter begins, I'll leave you with a quote from the great Dr. Brené Brown, whose works and words we'll explore throughout this chapter: "Because true belonging only happens when we present our authentic, imperfect selves to the world, our sense of belonging can never be greater than our level of self-acceptance" (Brown, 2010).

When Acceptance Has Conditions

I was raised in faith. I was baptized in a conservative Christian church, went to a parochial grade school, and attended a local Christian high school. In the tradition of the church, the importance of biblical and catechetical learning was emphasized. From my earliest memories, I had theology classes with our pastors, memorized passages from the Bible and the catechism, and openly talked about what it meant to be a "good" Christian. I loved church as a child – the hymns with the organ, the beautiful stained-glass windows, and the service filled with tradition spoke to something bigger and greater than myself. My faith filled me with a sense of wonder. I knew from an early age that I loved my faith, I was curious to know more, and I wanted to be active in the church.

Yet, in sixth grade, my understanding of our loving God was challenged. In our Human Growth and Development unit, our pastor addressed homosexuality for the first time. He claimed that two people of the same gender who engaged in sexual intercourse were gay, that homosexuality was an abomination, and all those living in this sin would go to hell. Now, in sixth grade, I knew that I was different from the other boys. When the pastor gave it the name, gay, I knew that he was talking to me. In that moment, it was expressed that the church that I loved didn't love me. The God whose love was unconditional had one condition that I knew I didn't meet.

I wish I could say that I felt my family offered me the support I needed in my childhood. Unfortunately, I felt the same judgment from them, as from my church. My parents said they loved me, and showed love in action – by coming to my games and concerts, by providing me and my brothers with a strong education, and by dedicating their energy to our success. However, in a family of boys, unspoken expectations of what it meant to "be a man" were very clear. From my perspective, my family, who were supposed to love me unconditionally, had the same condition as my God. I had no place in which I truly belonged – not at home, not at school, and not at church.

Growing up, I was a practical thinker and reasoned that if I had this sin that I couldn't get rid of, then I simply needed to be perfect in every other aspect of my life. I can remember being in grade school and truly believing that if I was the perfect student, athlete, son, Christian, then when others found out that I was gay, it wouldn't seem so bad, because I was so good in the rest of my life. I was an excellent student, a strong athlete, a talented artist.

I don't share these accomplishments to brag, but rather to emphasize what I went through to make sure everyone respected me, was impressed by me, and loved the me that I presented to them. Surely, everything that I did in school, in church, and at home would overshadow the fact that who I was inside was an "abomination." The denial of who I am was exhausting and, by the end of high school, I was done living a lie. When deciding on a college, I knew I wanted to go far away from my home. I wanted to find a place where I could come out of the closet and express my true self. It was at the University of Denver that I began to find a sense of belonging and started my journey of self-acceptance.

I was introduced to the Evangelical Lutheran Church in America (ELCA) while at college and was excited to discover a denomination that upheld the Lutheran doctrine while being open to and affirming of a wide diversity of people. For the first time in a long time, I stopped praying for God to make me straight and prayed for God's truth to be revealed in my life. With the guidance of my wonderful ELCA college pastor and the grace of God, I felt the weight of my struggle lifted from my shoulders. The sense of peace that came upon my heart and mind cannot be fully understood by those who have not been through a similar transformation. In my early adulthood at college, I went from a young man struggling to understand how God and others could love such an abomination, to a person of stronger faith, who came to know the assurance of God's unconditional love, the truth about who I am and how God created me, and the importance of having a place to belong in young people's lives.

I am happy to say that the fears I had growing up have been overcome. My family and friends fully love and affirm my created identity. I am especially blessed to have an extremely close relationship with my father and mother. I am close to my brothers and a fun-loving uncle of their children. And I have so many close friends that I truly consider to be family and love them as much as they love me. It turns out that my family, my friends, and my God did have one condition…for me to come, as I am, to receive their unconditional love. Turns out I always had a place to belong – it just needed to be revealed a bit more intentionally.

It Goes Without Saying

I have had the opportunity to share the story of my experiences as a "closeted" gay child with many audiences and I always want to make sure one thing is clearly known – my parents, teachers, coaches, friends are *all* wonderful, loving people. They were simply unaware of how societal, cultural, and in my case, religious norms created spaces of exclusion, doubt, and fear. My parents told me they loved me all the time. In fact, when I came out to my mom, she cried, not because I was gay, but because I thought that she would stop loving me because of it. Her unconditional love, in her mind, went without saying. When she and my father told me they loved me, they meant they loved me no matter what. The problem with assuming an understanding of unconditional love is that the world is constantly screaming its conditions – do more, have more, be more.

In the next chapter, I talk about speaking affirmations about oneself out into the world to help build and sustain confidence. Yet, as we'll see in the research, our internal voice is deeply connected to the external voices in our lives. As the world demands more, we must be the voices in our children's lives that assure them that they are enough. Yes, we can encourage them to strive to be their very best self, but we must always remind them that they are worthy, they are valued, they are loved – no matter what. It doesn't go without saying. It must be said and said often – the things that make you different are beautiful. Your entire identity is affirmed and embraced, exactly the way you are. Nothing will ever change the fact that you are worthy of love.

My Calling

Because of my experience with the church when I was growing up, I have always felt a strong calling to be an active member within my faith community, speaking up for the LGBTQIA+ community and speaking against the discrimination so often experienced by queer individuals by those claiming to be people of faith. I have led youth groups, Confirmation classes, and Sunday school lessons. I am an ordained pastor within the ELCA and I have had the honor of serving a congregation. In every faith community in which I have served, I have intentionally sought to speak words of inclusion, affirmation, and love. It was an easy choice to reach out to Brittany, one of my former youth, who identifies as queer. I cannot fully express how happy I am to know that she always felt loved and affirmed.

For most kids who identify on the LGBTQIA+ spectrum, church doesn't seem like the first place that they think of when they think of a place of belonging. For me and my other queer friends, church has always been a safe space. A safe space is defined as "a place or environment in which a person or category of people can feel confident that they will not be exposed to discrimination, criticism, harassment, or any other emotional or physical harm." The walls of my church, especially in terms of the youth group, have always been one of those places. When I came out, I was met with love and words of affirmation. That message was passed on to my friends when they started coming out at church. These words of affirmation came from staff members, pastors, youth group leaders, and even other youth group members. Even outside of the youth group, I found affirmation in our faith community and the greater ELCA denomination when sitting with over 30,000 of my siblings in Christ during the National Youth Gathering.

When talking about words of love and affirmation within the walls of my faith community, it came in different ways. It came in the form of jokes told by me and my friends. Jokes about coming out of the closet – for reference, we have a closet in our youth room and we loved to make that joke every time one of the queer youth group members walked out of it. Affirmation came in silly, yet supportive memes about our youth group and about Pastor Adam, our gay pastor. Those words also came in more serious sermons preached by Pastor Adam. I remember Pastor Adam preaching during Pride Month about queer pride and about how we should spread that love. That same day, I went and spread his affirming words via Facebook and at my local Pride Event. I could keep going with these little stories about our youth group and how loving and affirming it is. I could probably tell you hours upon hours of stories about silly little jokes, share TikToks about our youth group, and share about the very serious conversations that I've had with other youth group members, with Pastor Adam, and with other congregation members, but that would be enough to write my own book. So, I'll just say this – because of church, I know that I am loved just the way I am and I am thankful to have a place where I belonged.

Reflecting on Your Story

♦ What is your story? How did the words or actions of others affect your sense of belonging when you were in school?

♦ Where have you felt the safety to be yourself, to explore who you are, or to try being something new or different?

♦ Do you identify with a community that has traditionally faced discrimination? How have people in your life strengthened or hindered your sense of worth, value, and/or inclusion?

♦ When told that *you* have implicit biases that make your classroom unwelcoming and perhaps unsafe for some students, what is your initial reaction? If defensive, how can you explore shifting to a mindset that allows for difficult reflection and needed honesty?

Exploring Our "WHY"

All Means All

OK – so I have shared my story of being gay and I have shared the story of one of my queer youth from church, but please, realize that I am not simply talking about the inclusion of our LGBTQIA+ students. I am speaking about creating a loving and affirming space of belonging for *all* of our students. In order to effectively do this, we must raise our awareness of those who are most at risk of being excluded, who have been traditionally marginalized within our community, and who daily face biases and discrimination. Certainly, the queer community falls into this category, as do our students of color. But when you stop and truly observe your school community, who else is pushed to the margins and how does your classroom speak up for these students, affirm their presence in your class, proclaim their value, and ensure their belonging?

- Does your school have students who use a "nickname" rather than their birth name because it is easier for others to pronounce?
- Does your school assign advisory groups or homerooms based on assumed binary gender labels – girls and boys?
- Does your school celebrate Christmas, but not other religious holidays?
- Does your school mascot portray racist imagery?
- Does the office refer to students' guardians as "parents" or "mom and dad" when needing to call or email home?
- Are your school's playground and auditorium accessible to students of all physical abilities?

English-language learners, students of color, differently abled individuals, female-identifying students, members of the queer community, first-nation students, and students of non-Christian faith communities often face both implicit bias and direct discrimination within their schools. These students come to your classroom with armor that they have learned to put on each morning to protect themselves from harm as best they can. Before we can expect these students to open up, explore who they are, and discover all that they can become, we must offer a place of belonging that allows them to safely begin to remove this armor.

Belonging to Oneself

In her book *Braving the Wilderness: The Quest for True Belonging and the Courage to Stand Alone*, Dr. Brené Brown explores an understanding that we cannot seek belonging from others before discovering and developing a sense of belonging within ourselves. That is to say, "belonging to yourself so deeply that you can share your most authentic self with the world" (Brown, 2017). Doesn't that sound amazing – and shouldn't we want to empower our students with such a deep sense of true belonging that they can boldly stand up and share their authentic selves with the world?

So, if true belonging is internal, how can we, as teachers, guide our students to self-discovery and nurture this essential perspective. For that, I would suggest exploring another of Dr. Brown's incredible books, *The Gifts of Imperfection: Let Go of Who You Think You're Supposed to Be and Embrace Who You Are*. This book offers some great "guideposts" we can use in our own lives and which can be adapted to support our students in "cultivating" their sense of "true belonging." These guideposts sound a lot like our Keys of PDL. Brown encourages cultivating innate skills such as a resilient spirit and creativity, as well as authenticity (Confidence), laughter, song, and dance (Enthusiasm), calm and stillness (Focus), and self-compassion (Self-Empathy). Brown also offers her readers powerful action steps for letting go of the things that hinder one's sense of belonging – letting go of such things as perfectionism, comparison, self-doubt, being cool, and needing control (Brown, 2010). Sound like any students you know – I know that these very obstacles challenged my students on a daily basis. By focusing on the social-emotional health and well-being of our students, we are actually helping them to develop a strong, internal sense of true belonging. It's

Intentional Belonging ◆ 33

not easy – but it is certainly worth being an intentional focus of our classrooms and in our teaching.

Moving Beyond Just Safe

In schools, we talk about inclusivity, but often only go as far as emphasizing a "bully-free" zone. I would imagine that most teachers reading this book would confidently be able to say that no active bullying occurs within their classroom. When a student is overtly disrespectful or downright mean to another student, it is addressed. While this may be an important first step, creating a space of belonging requires more than the absence of intentional meanness. Stopping bullying and carrying out consequences for hurtful words and behaviors certainly makes one classroom safer for all students. Yet stepping up on Maslow's Hierarchy of Needs from safety to belonging requires intentional connection, inclusion, vulnerability, and engagement. As we'll explore toward the end of the book, our goal, once our students know they belong, is to help them self-assess – reaching the pinnacle of the hierarchy, self-actualization. We cannot settle for simply "achieving" the bottom of the pyramid (Maslow, 1943).

As teachers, we must move from welcoming our students into our learning environment to inviting them to create this space with us. We must grow from tolerance, beyond acceptance, to the affirmation of our students' authentic identities, passions, and expressions. As an inclusive space, a safe and supportive space – a space of belonging invites our students into a community that will affirm and value their worth regardless of differences. Our schools need to become communities that will affirm and value our students' worth regardless of productivity, grades, or achievement. *All* of our students are worthy. Our classrooms need to be spaces where they *all* belong.

Culturally Responsive Teaching

The world is changing – perhaps a timeless truth, the world has always and will continue to change. As it changes, we gain awareness, we must unlearn old ways, and open ourselves to new ways of understanding. What is true in our classrooms today has always been and will continue to be true. Our students come from diverse backgrounds, enter our classrooms with diverse needs, will engage in their learning with diverse perspectives, and can contribute to the class community in many diverse and beautiful ways. A standardized way of teaching can no longer be enough. Speaking to and hearing from a homogeneous collection of voices is not enough. The status quo, the way things "always have been done," and traditional teaching is *not* enough – probably was never enough. We can no longer claim ignorance or a lack of awareness of the need for diversity, equity, and inclusion within our classrooms and our schools.

We must be willing to acknowledge the lives of our students beyond our classrooms, allow them the opportunity to voice their own experiences, and empower them to find their own connections and meaning to their learning. We need to offer a diverse representation of voices and perspectives for our students through the readings, lessons, and guests we present to them. And we must work with families and our greater community in the development of our students so that we can work collaboratively in the growth of the whole child both within and beyond school walls.

Cherese Childers-McKee, an assistant teaching professor in Northeastern University's College of Professional Studies, in an article about Culturally Responsive Teaching, offers five strategies for educators (Burnham, 2020). We know the importance of building authentic, trusting relationships, which is one of her suggestions. Yet she also encourages teachers to use the diverse cultural experiences and perspectives of our students to help "hook" their interest and "anchor" their learning. She reminds us how powerful it can be to have the students become the teacher, offering their expertise and "cultural capital" – sharing with others their unique experiences. Finally, Childers-McKee encourages us to take an intentional look at our classrooms, everything from the materials we read and hand out to the posters on our walls and the books on our shelves. Do these things celebrate the rich diversity of our schools? Can students see themselves and others like them represented in and through these things? Can other students grow in awareness and appreciation for those not like themselves through their engagement with these things? A culturally responsive classroom, like a Purpose-Driven classroom, is intentional.

Moving Beyond Safe Choices

Many teachers have sought to make their classroom safe and supportive – yet, without continual reflection and education, we can fall victim to becoming comfortable with a "good enough" mentality of inclusion and belonging. Without even knowing it, microaggressions and implicit biases can begin to make our students feel unsafe, under-valued, and excluded. I am sure, you are saying to yourself, I would never reject a child. I believe that many of you would never openly or intentionally exclude a child. Yet, in so many small ways, our implicit biases reject aspects of others' identities without us even realizing it. Microaggressions speak to an unconscious status of acceptance our students must achieve. It takes intentional and often very difficult self-reflection to begin to become aware of our divisive words and actions.

Implicit bias and microaggressions often reveal themselves through subtle surprise and words intended as compliments. Being surprised that a student of color is "articulate" or that a young gay male student is "good at sports" are examples. Complimenting the "professional" look of a female student of color when her hair is pulled back rather than left natural or praising a student who is differently abled for completing a task like the "regular" students are additional examples. There is often surprise when a person from a minority community "acts" like those in the majority. Compliments and praise are offered when people within these marginalized communities begin to assimilate and "act" more like the majority. I believe that for many of us these words and actions are unintentional – yet, without realizing it, we are saying that these students are not enough or, perhaps more accurately, we are communicating that they are better, more acceptable, more valued when they behave, speak, or look a certain way, like those in communities of power and privilege. Such microaggressions and biases may not seem "that bad" – but when aspects of your students' identities are regularly dismissed, ignored, or require alteration, there cannot be a sense of belonging and you risk affirming a need for your students to reject part of who they are in order to blend in, rather than belong.

If you are unfamiliar with the concept of microaggression and implicit bias or would like to learn more, I strongly encourage you to educate yourself on these topics with authors far more equipped to teach you about these challenging topics. I would suggest *Beyond Conversations About Race: A Guide for Discussions With Students, Teachers, and Communities* – a powerful book with contributions by a number of diverse authors (Collado et al., 2021). Also, Benson and Fiarman's *Unconscious Bias in Schools: A Developmental Approach to Exploring Race and Racism* (Benson and Fiarman, 2019) and Wing Sue's *Microaggressions in Everyday Life: Race, Gender, and Sexual Orientation* (Wing Sue, 2010) – these books tackle hard subjects in practical and accessible ways. We must continue to grow past where we currently feel comfortable in order to help our students grow beyond boundaries of their own making and the making of our school system, culture, and society.

Inspiring Our Students' Stories

- ◆ Can you list some of the various cultures and communities in which your students identify?
- ◆ Can your students see themselves or their culture within the classroom materials with which they engage (books, handouts, research, posters, etc.)?
- ◆ When in a given lesson and/or school day do students have the opportunity to express their authentic self and/ or the communities in which they identify?
- ◆ How are the diverse cultures and communities represented in your student body celebrated, affirmed, and valued within your classroom and school?

Unlocking and Empowering Purpose-Driven Belonging

An Essential Contribution

The most important voices to empower within your classroom are the voices of your students. Not just their voices, but what their voices are sharing, expressing, contributing. How often have you asked for student feedback on a lesson, unit, or your teaching? Ah, an even more challenging question – how did your students' feedback change the lesson, unit, or your teaching? Sure, there are teachers who don't even ask for their students' contribution. To those teachers, I say – let your students contribute in a meaningful way to their learning within your classroom. However, I suspect that many teachers allow for their students' contributions. To these teachers, I ask – how does your students' contribution to their learning impact your teaching? In my experience, a sense of belonging is closely connected to a sense that one's contribution matters. It is natural for our students to ask what difference their presence makes at school and within our classrooms. Do you have a truly honest and meaningful response for your students? Now, it might not be every day, in every class, but our students must feel that their presence and contribution matter. So ask them questions about their learning and request feedback about your teaching – then, apply their contributions in authentic and impactful ways.

What's in a Name

"Voice and Choice" is nothing new. It is one of those educational buzz phrases thrown around all the time. As we explore belonging, we must ask – what does empowering our students' voices really look like? For me and the various groups of young people with whom I work, voice begins with sharing one's name with confidence. Do you know how many kids are willing to let someone call them by the wrong name, instead of speaking up and correcting them? Our name is our identifier. It is how we are acknowledged, how we declare our presence, and how we differentiate our contributions. The least a teacher can do – and I do mean the very least a teacher must do – is know their students' names.

From the first day of classes, camp, or youth group, even within the classes I substitute teach, I ask that everyone shares with me and the group their name – confidently and clearly. I speak their name and check to make sure I am pronouncing it correctly if it is a challenging name for me. I do not let them let me off the hook – "Close enough" or "Just call me [insert easier name]."

Many students' names have common nicknames: William to Billy or Jennifer to Jenny. I ask my students what they would like me to call them and I don't take "whatever" or "I don't care" for an answer. This is your name – own it and declare it with pride!

Now I am not some name guru – and sometimes, I have to humbly ask for their name again, apologize if I forget, or change when they decide to be called something new – so many middle school girls experiment with their name: Elizabeth, Lizzie, Beth, Liz, Eliza, Betsy, Libby. The name Ishan can be pronounced in at least three different ways. And don't get me started with the same name all spelled differently: Caileigh, Kailey, and Kaylee. It can be challenging when the name is not one that we are culturally familiar with – I never mess up names like Matt, Lily, Joey, or Grace. But I have had students whose names I personally found challenging when first introduced, yet names that once intentionally learned were no more challenging than the names I had already been familiar with. Take the time, put forth the effort. It can be a lot to keep track of, but identifying our students by name is essential in building a space where they feel seen, known, and valued.

A Word of Warning

A sense of belonging is a delicate thing – like a trusting relationship, it takes intentionality, effort, and time to build. Yet a single careless word or action can cause it great harm. Unfortunately, using the fear of losing one's belonging is a "discipline" tactic often used by schools. When grades are not high enough, students lose the opportunity to participate in extracurriculars. These after-school activities are where many of our students find a strong sense of belonging – on their sports teams, part of their clubs, within their arts ensembles. These are the times throughout the day when they can be with like-minded peers who share their interests, they can learn from adults who share their passion, and they can demonstrate their skills in areas in which they can truly shine. It is at these times our students can be their most authentic selves. And yet it is these times that are seen as "extra" and able to be taken away to "encourage" a change in effort or behavior.

We know that there are exceptional benefits to increasing our students' sense of belonging. Equally as true is the damage schools can cause by stripping away these students' sense of belonging as a consequence. Fear and isolation are not effective disciplinary actions. Now, I am not saying that students can't be held accountable. Certainly, if their words or actions are creating an unsafe or unwelcoming space for others, they may need to be removed until they can reflect on how their behavior is affecting others' sense of belonging – like the hazing of underclassmen on a sports team or the divisive actions of a lead "diva" in the musical. Temporary removal may also be needed to help students reflect and connect their words and actions between the various areas in their life – why is it that they put forth their best effort on the basketball court, but not in the math classroom? Why is it that the debate team can count on them to prepare for the meet, but their science lab partner is left to do all the work themselves? It's not that they're lazy. It's not that they're unreliable. They simply need support in seeing the connection and becoming more consistent in their demonstration of key social-emotional learning skills. Taking away the opportunities to demonstrate skills such as effort, focus, and dependability does not mean they will magically become better in the area in which they are struggling. It means that, in their school days, the time in which they feel the best about themselves, have the most support, and feel the greatest sense of belonging has been taken – and that is sad and ineffective. We can – we must – do better.

Proactive Rather Than Reactive

In my time as a congregational pastor, I often talked with my congregation about moving beyond being a community willing to change to being a community that proactively prepares to grow. It's a small shift in one's mindset that can have a huge impact within one's community. As you look over your class roster and come across names that are challenging, reach out to these students' teachers from the previous semester or year and see if they can help you learn names before the students ever step foot in your classroom. You don't need a student who publicly identifies as transgendered or non-binary in your class in order to encourage students to share their pronouns during introductions. How would a visiting student in a wheelchair navigate your classroom? How can you intentionally offer a perspective from a marginalized community in your next lesson?

As humans, we often are resistant to "forced" change. Yet, as teachers, we tend to be pretty good at adapting and growing with each new year and new classroom of children. So – prepare, be proactive. For your own peace of mind, don't wait to be forced, adapt now. Little steps at your own pace, so that you won't be forced to jump into the deep end when it becomes a necessity. More than yourself, do it for your students, both for those you have now and those you will have in the future. Imagine the sense of welcome a student will feel when you become the first teacher who pronounces their name correctly on the first day. Imagine the sense of inclusion a student will feel when books written in Spanish are available in your classroom library. Imagine the deep sense of belonging your students will discover when they see themselves represented, have opportunities to contribute their voices, and are affirmed for simply sharing their authentic selves with the world.

References

Benson, T. and Fiarman, S. (2019). *Unconscious Bias in Schools: A Developmental Approach to Exploring Race and Racism*. Cambridge, MA: Harvard Education Press.

Brown, B. (2017). *Braving the Wilderness: The Quest for True Belonging and the Courage to Stand Alone*. New York: Random House.

Brown, B. (2010). *The Gifts of Imperfection: Let Go of Who You Think You're Supposed to Be and Embrace Who You Are*. Center City: Hazelden Publishing.

Burnham, K. (2020). *Culturally Responsive Teaching: 5 Strategies for Educators*. Northeastern University Graduate Programs. Retrieved 16 November 2021, from www.northeastern.edu/graduate/blog/culturally-responsive-teaching-strategies/.

Collado, W., Hollie, S., Isiah, R., Jackson, Y., Muhammad, A., Reeves, D. and Williams, K. (2021). *Beyond Conversations about Race: A*

Guide for Discussions with Students, Teachers, and Communities. Bloomington: Solution Tree Press.

Maslow, A. H. (1943). A theory of human motivation. *Psychological Review*, *50*(4), 370–396. https://doi.org/10.1037/h0054346.

Wing Sue, D. (2010). *Microaggressions in Everyday Life: Race, Gender, and Sexual Orientation*. 1st ed. Hoboken: Wiley.

3

The Key of Confidence: The Journey of Becoming

Connecting to My Story

A Theatrical Becoming

"Places, places," the stage manager whispers from the wings. You step out on stage and stand just right of center, facing the curtain that begins to rise. There are butterflies in your stomach, your pulse is racing, and you take a breath. The curtain is raised above you and you can, for only a moment, see out into the audience. It is a full house. As far as you can see, every seat is taken. Yet, before you can look more closely, the lights come up. A void of darkness swallows the audience, and in your mind, you visualize the fourth wall, the world you and the cast will create on stage for the next two hours. Nervousness is replaced with an energy that drives the words and actions of each scene. There is a theatrical "becoming," as you become your character and the stage becomes the world of the play.

Before you know it, the last line is spoken, the last song sung, the last step danced, the last note played. There is the briefest moment of silence, a precious instant between what has happened and what is about to occur, a silent colliding of two worlds. The performance is over, your work is complete, and the audience erupts into applause, clapping and cheering for the

DOI: 10.4324/9781003294634-4

artistry they just witnessed, they just experienced. You stand on stage under the spotlight and are, at least for this moment, a star who is appreciated and adored by all who are present. A rush of emotions floods over you. There is a feeling of accomplishment as two months of rehearsals have paid off. There is a sense of pride, as you have done something so many fear doing. There is the slightest sense of sadness, as soon it will all be over. And there is, above all else, a sense of overwhelming joy, for you have come to love all that theatre has to offer. In this moment, there is no other place you want to be, no other thing you would rather do. And before a standing ovation, you take a bow.

The Act of Becoming

There is something truly unique about theatre. There are many activities we try that we like, that we do for a little while, but then we stop. Music lessons end, we try out for different sports, or we find a new hobby that captures our interest. Yet theatre is different. Theatre transforms people. The act of "becoming" is not simply on stage as the actor becomes the character. It is an act of a person becoming someone different than they thought they could be, becoming someone bigger and bolder, becoming someone more confident in who they are, willing to share that person with the world. I know, it all sounds a little dramatic, but it's true.

As an actor, I have experienced this "becoming" first hand as I discovered a passion for theatre in my high school years. I did not grow up in a theatrical family, nor did I have any dreams of starring in a musical. I grew up with two brothers and we all played sports. It's not that I want to perpetuate a stereotype that athletes can't also be artists, or artists can't be athletes. In fact, my brothers and I were involved in music. My older brother played the French horn, I played the trumpet, and my younger brother played the cello. It's not that my parents were against the arts or that my dad fit some stereotype of a blue-collar "man's man" who only wanted his sons to do "manly" things. No, not at all – it was simply that they had not been involved in theatre or raised attending theatre, so it was not something we did in my family. In the fall, we played football. In the winter, we wrestled. In the spring, we played Little League baseball. And my dad coached all of our sports up until high school. We were mainly a sports family and had little time for other extra-curricular activities.

As I followed my brother into high school, I played the sports he played, the sports we grew up playing. That is, until my sophomore year. In my second year of high school, I played football and was selected to play on the varsity team. I wrestled and qualified for the Wisconsin State Tournament. Then, in the spring, instead of baseball, something different, something very unexpected, caught my eye: the Spring Musical.

Yes, very much like Troy Bolton in *High School Musical*, I made the leap from athlete to musical actor as I auditioned for *Fiddler On The Roof*. Unlike in the beloved Disney movie musical, I did not get the lead in the first production I ever auditioned for. I got a chorus role and had exactly one speaking line. My involvement did not cause the cafeteria to erupt into song and choreographed dance as the cast was announced, nor were my sports buddies upset with me "boldly" breaking down social cliques within the school. No, my involvement as male chorus member #7 went relatively unappreciated and unfortunately did not radically change the entire school community. However, as I took on the role and experienced theatre for the first time, I was radically changed.

Every day after school for two months, I worked on becoming someone else, someone with a backstory, a life much different than my own. I rehearsed with the other performers in the ensemble, working to transform our American, Midwest, middle-class world into the world of Anatevka, a poor Russian village, a world so much different than our own. Throughout this process, and more specifically through this process, a passion sparked inside of me, a love for theatre, and a confidence in my ability to walk out on the stage in front of hundreds of people and share a piece of myself. This confidence took root, and as the show came to an end, the audience cheered and clapped for my performance. Well, the audience cheered and clapped for the per-formance of the whole ensemble…solo bows would come much later in my acting career. Yet, in that first experience, it didn't matter that I bowed with the chorus, that my individual efforts were not singled out. Rather, the work of the whole ensemble, cast and crew, was celebrated. We had created something truly amazing and confidently shared it with the world; well, shared it with our world. Our family and friends, our teachers and classmates celebrated how far we came. However, my journey of becoming something new, something more, something different, had just begun.

As shared in the opening chapter, I would go on to pursue theatre in college and dabble in professional theatre right after I graduated, before accepting a teaching position as the middle school Drama teacher at University School of Milwaukee. While the process of becoming is a lifelong journey, for a time I was quite content with who I had become. I sought to help children and teens discover and explore their own journeys of becoming their very best selves, their journeys of becoming who they were created to be. In my years of teaching and directing, I have witnessed, time and time again, what I had experienced way back in high school: the transformative power of theatre.

Research reveals what many of us know to be true: Public speaking is a majority of people's number one fear. Not heights, not spiders, not clowns, not even death – that's right, a whole lot of people would rather die getting pushed off a skyscraper by a spider in a clown wig than get up and perform in front of an audience, and I kinda get it. When you're dead, it's done, but after a performance, you have to face the feedback of friends, family, colleagues, and, many times, complete strangers. So as my fifth graders would come up into middle school and have Drama for the first time, I understood the anxiety and fear that accompanied them.

My role as a Drama teacher, especially in fifth grade, was not to cause shame around their fears or make them feel foolish for being scared; nor was my role to make excuses for their fears and allow those fears to prevent them from performing. No, my role was to help them acknowledge their fear, confront it, and throughout their time in middle school, overcome it. While I truly have countless stories of students who boldly took risks, who accepted the challenges of performing with confidence, and who continually exceeded my expectations, I want to share two stories of former students who have given permission to share their experiences. In seeking permission to share their stories, it was wonderful to reconnect with Nathan and Lizzie, hear about where they are now in their journeys, and how they still consider the lessons they learned in middle school Drama to be valuable in their young adult lives.

Fear as Obstinance

Nathan was a great student. Well, Nathan was a great student in the traditional setting of an academic classroom. He knew how to play the game we call "school." He was and still is very smart and incredibly focused. Even at ten years old, he was confident in his intelligence, knowing that when push came to shove, he could always figure out the "right" answer. And then Nathan walked into Mr. Moreno's middle school Drama classroom.

This was the world of theatre – in the arts, there are very few, if any, "right" answers. Improvisation games and ensemble-building exercises test creativity, spontaneity, trust, and teamwork like no standardized test ever could – and nothing was graded! Rubrics came to them blank and asked them to fill in what they wanted to be assessed on. The question "what do we have to do to get an A" had no answer, because Drama wasn't about getting a good grade. In my classroom, it was about being better than your last performance – doing your best was expected and the students got to define what their best was and how successful they were at meeting their Purpose-Driven Learning (PDL) objectives. The Drama classroom was anything but "traditional" and Nathan was faced with something completely unfamiliar.

Now a confident, incredibly bright student rarely admits fear when confronted with the challenges Nathan faced. No, instead of confessing uncertainty or apprehension, he articulated his feelings as eloquently as a ten-year-old could: Drama was dumb and he hated it. Seriously, in a story he and his mother tell, he got into the car after his first day of Drama class and told his mom that he didn't want to take Drama because it was a "waste of his time." In that first semester of fifth grade, he admits to dreading the days he had Drama.

Nathan claimed he didn't like it, but as a teacher, I knew that the underlying cause of his resistance was rooted in fear and a lack of confidence in his abilities. This uncertainty was a new experience for Nathan and it was my role as his teacher to guide and encourage him. Now any of my former students will tell you that my teaching style is not exactly warm and fuzzy. The best way I have found to overcome fear is to attack it head-on. A common saying in my Drama classroom was, "Everyone participates because everyone participates." There was no "passing," no "I'll do it next time," or "just skip me." The expect-ation was set that everyone needed to participate, and because everyone participated, everyone participated. Nathan knew he had to jump in, he had to play, he had to participate. In doing so, he came to realize that Drama wasn't so bad. His confidence grew because he took the needed risks, he confronted his fears, he demonstrated his abilities, and he challenged himself to improve.

And improve he did – in the classroom and in our after-school plays and musicals. In sixth grade, he was a pirate in Treasure Island, in seventh grade, he was Tweedle Dum (pun intended) in *Alice In Wonderland*, and in eighth grade, the little boy who "hated" Drama tried out for the musical *Annie* and earned the lead male role of Daddy Warbucks. As Nathan sang and danced and acted, all could see that in his journey of becoming, he had confidently taken giant strides.

Fear as Doubt

Now Lizzie was a lot like Nathan, very smart and really a strong student in the more traditional academic classrooms. And while, like Nathan, Lizzie struggled with confidence in the Drama classroom, her fears fed a narrative of "not being good enough." She compared herself to others and believed that she would never measure up. This lack of confidence caused her to miss out on opportunities to challenge herself, to grow, and to have the experiences that would grow her confidence. In fifth grade, she didn't try out for the play or musical, which makes sense. If you feel like you have no talent, then why set yourself up for failure?

This is where it is truly a blessing that my students had a required Drama program in middle school. Even though she didn't participate in the theatre extracurricular, Lizzie did work hard in Drama class throughout fifth grade. She took action – bravely jumping into improvisation games like "Everybody Go" and acting silly in front of her classmates. She fully participated in the development, rehearsals, and performances of her fifth-grade Fable and Shakespeare Fight Scene, showing that she was a dependable ensemble member who could be trusted to contribute her best and perform her role. And at the beginning of sixth grade, she shined in the solo performance of her Superhero Monologue and took everyone by surprise with her confident and hilarious Stand-up Comedy Routine. In her journey of becoming, Lizzie took greater and greater risks and challenged herself to push the boundaries of her comfort zone in order to develop. With her developing confidence, she auditioned for the Spring musical, *The Sound of Music*, and earned the role of Brigitta. While this was a character very similar to herself, a rather soft-spoken bookworm, she made it her own, worked hard, and shared with a sold-out crowd what she had become… and it was wonderful!

Mr. Moreno,

Thank you doesn't seem to mean enough. I don't know whether it was just wanting to be perfect (which no one is) or me striving to get your approval that made me a better actor. You had confidence in me for my Comedy Routine in class, even when I didn't. You have placed, no planted, confidence deep within me. In time, it will bloom and grow just like edelweiss. Stagefright has always been a terrible barrier between me and my goals. I sat on the sidelines during Schoolhouse Rock and it made me think, "I wish I could have done that." Now I have the tool to go out and achieve my dreams. Last year my comfort zone didn't want to budge, but this year I feel that it has leapt a whole foot into new and exciting things I have yet to experience. As with a lot of things, acting was something I wasn't extremely good at so I didn't like it. But now I realize you can like something even if you're not good at it. Like making a batch of cookies, just as an example. I may not be amazing at baking cookies, but I enjoy it and that's what really matters. Hint: if I ever bake something, DON'T EAT IT! Can't wait till rehearsal on Tuesday. I've been working hard to memorize my lines. The script has become my new ORB [Optional Reading Book]. Haha!

Lizzie (Brigitta)

Lizzie wrote this letter during the rehearsal process for the musical in sixth grade, but her growth didn't stop there. In seventh grade, she beat out experienced and talented eighth-grade girls to earn the lead role of Sarah Brown in *Guys and Dolls*. And in eighth grade, to complete her middle school journey, she commanded the stage as Golde in a truly remarkable production of *Fiddler on the Roof*.

These two students were not the exception but were very much the incredible norm, as my middle school students were given the opportunity to experience that which so many fear: getting up in front of an audience and sharing a piece of themselves. Nathan and Lizzie participated in theatre throughout high school, and as they have journeyed beyond the walls of my classroom and beyond the stage of our theatre, they have taken the confidence discovered and developed with them into the world. Nathan shared these words with me as we reflected on his journey: *"Theatre helped me to realize that confidence doesn't equate to always having the right answer, but rather being able to trust my ability to attempt problems with imperfect solutions."* Perfectly said, Nathan.

Reflecting on Your Story

- ◆ In which of your talents do you feel the most confidence? How did you develop your confidence in this talent?
- ◆ When was the last time you did something for the first time?
- ◆ How do you react to new experiences? How do you handle experiences that you try and find you do not yet have the skills needed to succeed?

50 ◆ The Key of Confidence

- ◆ Can you recall ever doubting your abilities, talents, and skill set? Were you a beginner? Had you failed at something you thought you could achieve?
- ◆ Do you ever conflate confidence and arrogance? In your understanding, what is the difference between the two? How can one express confidence and humility?

Exploring Our "WHY"

Cornerstone Confidence

What are our students going to need to be successful in their lives? Reading, writing, and arithmetic…sure. 21st-century technology skills…yup. However, I would argue that one of the most important qualities we can develop in our students is confidence. Confidence, as far as leadership "success" is concerned, is arguably more important than knowledge. The research, by Dr. Don Moore of Carnegie Mellon University, suggests that a majority of people believe the words of a "confident source" over an "accurate source" (Barker, 2011). Now, as educators, I hope we can all agree that we want to develop confident *and* intelligent students who will become influential leaders in our world. Yet, if we can only choose one – just kidding, let's strive for both.

So, I have intentionally placed confidence as the first key to explore because of its "cornerstone-quality" for all other Keys of PDL. All of the keys connect in interesting and dynamic ways. Yet confidence, in my experience, directly connects in foundational ways to the rest as we seek to teach and develop these life skills. Our students must be confident in their abilities to focus on the task at hand and come up with creative solutions. When confronted with inevitable obstacles, they must be confident in their resilience, in order to continue to enthusiastically put forth their best effort in confronting and overcoming setbacks and failures. Confidence empowers students to take the initiative in their own learning and follow where their curiosity leads. Confidence allows our students to open up and express the vulnerability needed to collaborate with empathy and dependability.

The Power of Public Speaking

As we explore the Key of Confidence apart from its connection to the other keys, it is important to define what I mean by confidence. As a Drama teacher, I believe that overall confidence is discovered, developed, and demonstrated in and through performance, public speaking, and presentation. That is to say, when I speak of confidence, I am speaking of our students' abilities to publicly articulate who they are, what they believe, and how they understand the world. Developing confidence in my classroom, through my Drama program, and in all of my roles working with children, I seek to empower students to:

- ◆ Confidently express their learning and contribute their strengths
- ◆ Confidently admit what they don't know and acknowledge their limitations
- ◆ Confidently share their voice, speak up when needed, and stand their ground
- ◆ Confidently confront their fears and embrace a growth mindset
- ◆ Confidently take bold risks and push the boundaries of their comfort zone

A 2019 study of business and law students at the University of Portsmouth in England supports this understanding of performance and confidence. A required assignment of creating and presenting an "elevator pitch" of themselves for a hypothetical job interview revealed considerable improvement in what the researchers called the students' "employability-related self-confidence." The study also showed that the students were able to take this strengthened self-confidence and transfer it to different contexts. That is to say, the "performance" assignment in one class had an impact on other classes and other aspects of their lives (University of Portsmouth, 2014).

At any age, in every classroom, students need to be challenged to do more than just quietly sit and carefully listen. Students need to be expected to confidently share their thoughts, discuss differing opinions, and ask questions for deeper understanding. All teachers work hard to build their students' content knowledge; equally as important is the need to build students' ability to share this knowledge and express their learning publicly and with confidence.

Almost everyone reading this book is not a theatre teacher and your students are most likely not going to be Broadway or Hollywood stars. Yet, whether your students want to be lawyers, business people, doctors, cashiers at McDonald's, or even teachers, performance and presentation skills are essential skills for success. How far would Steve Jobs or Bill Gates have gone if they could not have expressed their brilliance with confidence? We see every election season the tragic result of candidates who seem incapable of speaking with intelligence and/or confidence. And don't get me started on professional athletes' post-game interviews…cringe! In all seriousness, public-speaking skills will help them stand out in school and in their jobs. They will help them speak up and have their voices heard as they seek to make an impact in the world. Confident public speaking, performance, and presentation skills will help them connect with others, will allow them to be strong and effective collaborators, and will empower them to be inspiring leaders. Confidence matters!

Inspiring Our Students' Stories

- ◆ How might you communicate the Key of Confidence as a cornerstone skill to your students?
- ◆ In what ways are your students given the opportunity to express who they are, what they believe, and how they understand the world?
- ◆ How well do your students confidently share their perspectives, discuss their learning, or ask questions when they don't understand?

Unlocking and Empowering Purpose-Driven Confidence

A Confidence-Centered Classroom

The first step in the journey of building a classroom on the foundation of confidence is an understanding of our own fears and exploring our own confidence. I can't tell you how many parents of my Drama students told me that they could never perform the way their kids perform on stage. My response is always the same: "You could if you were given the skills to do so!" I am even more surprised when teachers express the same fear. Come on, don't we stand up and "perform" in front of our classes every day? My colleagues say that it is different, and I couldn't agree more. Teenagers are way more judgmental than any audience I have ever performed for. When implementing confidence skill-building into your classroom, take a moment to reflect on your own thoughts and feelings about being up in front of an audience.

Take a Stand for Confidence

OK, so I have heard that not every classroom has time to perform. Perhaps there is some truth to that. However, every classroom has time to build public-speaking skills. When asked a question, I require my students to stand to offer their answers. This expectation takes no more time away from my class than having the students remain seated. By standing, the students can address the whole class, which takes quite a bit of confidence. Teachers with whom I have worked who implemented this strategy have found that, over time, their students speak with more authority when they are standing, the focus of the class shifts more fully to the person who is speaking, and the feel of classroom conversation becomes much more collaborative. Here are some additional thoughts that will help build confidence, especially as the students stand to offer their thoughts, their perspectives, and their learning.

My Eyes Are Up Here

Eye contact is essential! It is through the eyes that people connect with others. Whether coming in and shaking my hand at the start of class or sharing their thoughts in a class discussion, eyes need to be up, and the students need to be looking at the people they are addressing. If their eyes are down, I will ask students to repeat what they said while making eye contact with the class. Often, if a second time is needed, I will have the student speak directly to me instead of addressing the entire class. Only having one person to look at often comforts those students who are nervous to speak in front of the entire class.

Shy Is Not a Good Thing

There is a difference between being introverted and being shy. Yes, you will have introverts, and, of course, there is nothing wrong with how they process and express their learning. However, do not confuse it with being shy. Shy people "shy away" from risk, challenges, the unknown, and opportunities that may help them grow. Introverts may not love performing, they may truly feel anxious about sharing their learning aloud. Yet we expect our extroverted students to learn to sit quietly, reflect thoughtfully, and focus carefully. We can and need to challenge our introverted students to build their public-speaking skills. As teachers, we know the importance of these skills and how empowering they can be for *all* of our students.

Ummms, and Likes, Yeahs, and Stuff

In one of his powerful speeches, Winston Churchill once said, "It's quite simple. Say what you have to say and when you come to a sentence with a grammatical ending, sit down" (O'Brien, 2011). If Churchill had been a middle school girl, his quote may have sounded more like this: "Ahhhhhh…I mean, yeah, it's like super easy. Ummm, just think before you speak. And like say what like only needs to be said. Ummm…and like when you've shared your thoughts, ummmmm, like, yeah, stop talking and just like sit…and stuff."

Perhaps it's funny when written out, but nothing – and I mean, nothing – drives me crazier than "filler" words and sounds. I tell my students that when called on, they should stand, take a deep breath, and gather their thoughts. They should start by stating the question, then they should answer the question. Question: Who was the first president of the United States? Stand, breathe, and when ready speak: The first president of the United States was George Washington. And when they have given their complete answer, they sit. This gives clarity to the start of their answer. I have found that when students start their answers strong the answers are spoken with more confidence.

Random Really Isn't All That Random

Don't always call on the students with their hands up…they think they know the answer. Call on the students not raising their hands, who are avoiding eye contact in hopes they won't be noticed. Call on students in a pattern, then, without warning, break the pattern. Call on the "know-it-all" student when you know he doesn't know. Call on the quiet student when you know she does know. Have everyone write down the answer, switch papers, then share the answer as if it were their own. I know there are people who will want to use the heightened sense of anxiety as a reason to have an ordered system and not put students on the spot. Yet I have found that keeping students guessing on who is going to be called on next keeps them engaged and helps build public-speaking skills for all students, not just the ones with their hands up. Is it easy? No, none of this is, but we grow when we're uncomfortable and when the boundaries of our comfort zones are challenged.

No Passes

I get it – you are trying to be nice. You don't want to traumatize the poor children by "making" them speak in front of the class. You go around the classroom, but if a student doesn't feel comfortable contributing you allow them to "pass." I challenge you to ask yourself what you are letting them "pass" on. They are passing on the chance to share their thoughts. They are passing on the opportunity to get the right answer. They are passing on the opportunity to have their voice heard. They are passing on the chance to be a contributing part of the class. Every now and then I let a student "phone a friend" and call on a classmate to assist them. Every so often, I let a student with a "deer-in-the-headlights" look temporarily pass and I move on to another student, but they know that I am coming back to them after they have a chance to collect their thoughts. By letting no one pass, everyone is expected to be an active member of your classroom. When everyone is expected to participate – everyone participates!

"I Don't Know" – That's OK, but Still Expect an Answer

This might be my students' least favorite technique that I use and I love it. I ask a question and randomly call on a student, who responds with "I don't know." However, the students know that a response of "I don't know" is not allowed in my class. I reply with, "That's OK, but I still need an answer." Right or wrong, everyone has an answer. More often than not, the student knows the right answer, yet lacks the confidence to share it out of fear of being wrong. When the expectation of offering an answer is established, they really do give an answer. When it's right, I can offer confidence-building praise. If it is wrong, I can offer confidence-supporting encouragement. "Nope, that's not right, but that's OK. Let's figure out where the learning went in a different direction." Making the students offer an answer, no matter what, has two big benefits. One, students pay attention a lot closer because they don't want to give the wrong answer when called on. Two, it shows the students that giving the wrong answer isn't the end of the world. I don't like silly answers, but a reasonable answer that is the student's best guess is great and allows me to address a misunderstanding that others may have, as well. Whether right or wrong, I can praise the confidence it took to offer the answer.

Feel Their Pain…but Make Them Do It Anyway

Empathy is your friend. You know what they're going through; you have to get up in front of an "audience" every day and "perform." Don't say it's easy, because it's not for everyone. Don't claim that it's really tough, because the timid will not want to try. Focusing on building confidence is just something you are going to do because it is needed, period. Everyone can do it. Not everyone will like it. Some will succeed right away, others will struggle for a while, but it will benefit everyone who tries their hardest and puts forth their best effort. We don't apologize for making students read or write – don't apologize for striving to build their confidence through performance and public speaking. Confidence is an important tool for these students' educational toolbox.

The Power of Affirmations

A final and important strategy for building a confidence-centered classroom. Words are powerful. Your words of encouragement are needed and valuable. Yet, in our world, the voice most needing to be supportive and confident is our internal voice. Dr. Mark Leary, a professor of psychology at Wake Forest University and a distinguished researcher on the subject of self-confidence, found that an important determinant of self-confidence is developing a sense of "self-efficacy," meaning the belief that one is capable of facing challenges and completing tasks successfully (Walker, 2005).

Teachers of younger students are often very good at teaching self-affirmation. "Let's all say, I am awesome," and the little ones all join in the affirming class cheer. However, as students get older, we tend to think of speaking affirmation aloud as "childish." While teenagers might roll their eyes and even make fun of an intentional Affirmation Time, I cannot emphasize enough the importance of teaching the language of self-affirmation. So, give it a try – look in the mirror and tell yourself that you are awesome, beautiful, and more than enough. In her book *A Little Spot of Confidence*, Diane Alber offers these words as a powerful daily affirmation: "Today's a new day! I will have a great start. I will listen to the voice inside my heart. I will let good thoughts inside my mind and tell myself: I am brave, I am loving, I am kind" (Alber, 2019). What do you need to affirm about yourself? What do your students need to self-affirm? Have them turn their phones to "selfie" mode, look at themselves, and say aloud that they are confident, that they can overcome fear, that they are worthy to be heard. Acknowledge the awkwardness, but emphasize the importance and make them do it and do it often. It really can have a very meaningful impact. You can do this…*you are incredible*! Your students can do this…*they are amazing*!

References

Alber, D. (2019). *A Little SPOT of Confidence: A Story about Believing in Yourself*. Mesa: Diane Alber Art LLC.

Barker, E. (2011). *Do We Prefer Confidence or Expertise?*. Business Insider. Retrieved 11 August 2020, from www.businessinsider.com/do-we-prefer-confidence-or-expertise-2011-11.

O'Brien, T. (2011). *Little Red Book of Effective Speaking Skills*. New Delhi: Rupa Publications.

University of Portsmouth. (2014). *'Brand Me' Presentations Increase Students' Confidence and Enhance Their Employability*. Retrieved 22 August 2020, from www.port.ac.uk/news-events-and-blogs/news/brand-me-presentations-increase-students-confidence-and-enhance-their-employability.

Walker, C. (2005). *Psychologist Finds Self-Compassion Helps People Cope With Failure*. Wake Forest News. Retrieved 22 August 2020, from https://news.wfu.edu/2005/08/22/psychologist-finds-self-compassion-helps-people-cope-with-failure/.

4

The Key of Enthusiasm: Embracing a "Yes, I Can" Attitude

Connecting to My Story

The Beauty in Every Day

7:12am and it's a crisp morning toward the end of June in the Northwoods of Wisconsin. Throughout July and August, the air will warm into the dog days of summer, but at this hour of the day, this time of the year, this far up north, the chill moves in at night and clings tightly to the break of day. As the mist rises from the waters of Trout Lake in the quiet of the morning, it is not uncommon to see deer drinking from the lake, the red squirrels scurrying from tree to tree, or an eagle circling in the sky, looking for its breakfast.

Just fifty yards from the shore of the lake is the Quad of Red Arrow Camp. Once a logging company in the early 1900s, the authentic log cabins now house boys who are seven through sixteen years old for seven weeks every summer. As one stands in the middle of the Quad, they are surrounded by the cabins, the Rec Hall and Mess Hall, the Infirmary and Camp Office. Above them, one-hundred-year-old pines sway in the morning breeze; beneath their feet, a bed of soft pine needles carpets the ground. At 7:13am, standing in the empty Quad, if one listens close enough in the morning stillness, they may hear the echoes of yesterday's excitement and fun. Listen a little closer, and you may even hear the echoes of the joy of summers past, when the boys' fathers and grandfathers were at camp. These echoes stir the spirit of camp and prepare this place for yet another day of challenge, friendship, growth, and memories!

From the lake, to the Quad, one moves inside the cabins, where five wooden bunk beds line the walls. From these walls hang tennis rackets, lacrosse sticks, baseball caps, and slightly damp towels. Placed in the rafters are fishing poles, canoe paddles, waterskis, and, if you look closely, maybe you'll find a spiderweb or two. At the ends of each bed, there is a red kerchief folded into a triangle that tells the story of a boy's time at camp. If empty, the boy must be new and the emblems he will earn throughout the summer will not be sewn on until the fall. Yet other kerchiefs are filled with emblems and stars, and serve to communicate a boy's abilities in any given area of camp: a beginner in horseback riding, intermediate in woodshop, or possibly advanced in sailing. The longer a boy has been at camp, the more he has grown in his abilities and the kerchief becomes a treasured testament to his hard work, positive attitude, and perseverance.

In the beds, soundly asleep at 7:14am, are eight boys and two young men, totaling almost a hundred campers and twenty-four counselors in the twelve cabins throughout camp. A day at camp is filled with fun, but can be very, very tiring. A good night's sleep is essential for a great day. The seven- and eight-year-old boys seem so little as they cuddle with their stuffed animals. The teenagers, in comparison, seem so much bigger, as comedically large, bare feet dangle from the ends of beds. No matter the age of the campers in the cabin, as they sleep with the morning sun beginning to shine through the tree branches, into the windows, stretching across the wooden floors, there is a sense of anticipation and a promise of adventure as dreams come to an end and setting out to achieve those dreams is just moments away.

Ding, dong, ding, dong – the camp bell rings out at 7:15am sharp, breaking the silence and welcoming the day! It can be heard clear out to the Chateau where the oldest guys are slower to get up than the super energetic boys of Cabin A. But it's not

The Key of Enthusiasm ◆ 61

just the bell that the campers and counselors hear. No, as the ringing comes to an end, one can hear the old, familiar voice calling out the same morning wake-up that he has offered for over four decades.

Hey, hey, hey – everyone up. It's a beautiful day at Red Arrow!

Before his passing in 2012, Bob Krohn had been the director of Red Arrow Camp with his wife, Sue, for almost half of the camp's existence – forty-five of Red Arrow's ninety-two years. Every morning, he would walk up the path to the camp bell, and ring it long and loud at precisely 7:15am. After ringing the bell, he would go around to each cabin to greet them with "Good morning," and all along the way he would call out, "It's a beautiful day at Red Arrow!" It was a call that would let you know how close he was to your cabin, so you knew how long you had before needing to be up with your feet on the floor. It was also a call that assured you, at the start of every day, that this day was going to be a beautiful, a wonderful, a truly great day at camp.

Now, you may be thinking that on a gorgeous morning, such as the kind I just described, it would be easy to wake up with an enthusiastic and energetic attitude. And you're right, on the many sunny summer mornings of camp, a positive outlook is not too difficult. Getting up and getting ready for the day is easy-peasy, lemon-squeezy – but every morning is not a sunshiny, go-get-'em kind of morning.

7:12am and it's a bitterly cold morning toward the end of June in the Northwoods of Wisconsin. It's supposed to be summer, yet the ice on the lake wasn't completely melted until just three weeks ago. It's pouring rain and the waves on Trout Lake crash on the shore. Just fifty yards from the shore, up in the Quad, one can hear the wind howling through the pine trees. At 7:13am, standing there, looking at the cabins, one can see that everything out on the clotheslines, drying from the day before, is now soaking wet and huge puddles wash away the pine needles on the ground. From the lake, to the Quad, and at 7:14am, one moves inside the authentic log cabins and is acutely aware that they are from the early 1900's and don't have any heat. When it's cold, it is cold. In the younger cabins, the campers were up all night frightened of the thunderstorm, so the counselors have only gotten a couple of hours of sleep. And the older boys, who are the furthest away from the "8," lie awake needing to go to the bathroom, but not wanting to get soaked by the rain running there and back.

Ding, dong, ding, dong – the camp bell rings out at 7:15am sharp, breaking through the sound of the rain beating on the roof. But it's not just the rain and the bell that the campers and counselors hear. No, as the ringing comes to an end, one can hear the old, familiar voice calling out the same morning wake-up that he has offered for over four decades.

Hey, hey, hey – everyone up. It's a beautiful day at Red Arrow!

What? A beautiful day at Red Arrow? The weather is horrible and almost everyone is going to be cold, wet, tired, and miserable. How can this guy expect us to believe that today, of all days, is going to be a beautiful day? I have to admit that on these "less-than-beautiful" mornings, I was skeptical of Bob's enthusiasm. I wanted to pull my blankets over my head, ignore the whining of my campers, and wait out the storm. But that's not the attitude Bob shared, as he called out, "It's a beautiful day at Red Arrow!"

Here's the thing about Bob – he wasn't crazy. His somewhat confounding optimism wasn't because he was delusional. No, Bob knew it was cold and rainy. He was fully aware that the day ahead was going to pose a number of challenges: mud in the Mess Hall, classes and planned activities canceled, and less than enthusiastic campers and staff. Yet Bob also knew and put into practice a truth that so many of us often forget: There are things beyond our control, but we need to focus on the things within our control, like our response to challenges, surprises, and unexpected situations. We cannot control the weather, but we can control our reaction to the weather.

At camp, we have a common saying: "Yes, I Can." These three words are on a big sign that hangs on the outside of the Rec Hall that can be seen throughout the Quad. It is a motto that reminds us that we can accomplish anything we set out to do

The Key of Enthusiasm ◆ 63

with determination, teamwork, and a positive attitude. Bob's "Yes I Can" attitude, his enthusiastic energy, was a choice. True, it was an easier choice on the sunny days, but it was just as important, if not more important, on the cold and rainy days. As the leader of camp, he knew that his attitude would impact everyone, so he chose a positive and enthusiastic attitude and shared it with every camper and counselor at the start of the day, rain or shine, each and every day.

While his "Yes I Can" attitude was certainly an intentional choice of a wise leader, I don't think that on those gray days Bob was faking enthusiasm simply to inspire us. I believe that he truly believed that every day at Red Arrow was a beautiful day. In his early years at camp, perhaps Bob simply had faith that everything was going to work out and that the day, no matter how stormy, would end with a rainbow, and hope for a better day tomorrow. Yet, after 45 years, Bob's enthusiasm was not simply a matter of faith. It was rooted in experience. Unexpected change, while challenging, brought new possibilities, a break from the normal routine, and the opportunity to come together as a community. Bob was confident that, even though the plans for the day would need to change, the beauty of camp would simply be revealed in different ways.

In my mere two decades connected to Red Arrow, I can attest to the accuracy of his wisdom. Sunny days meant we could be outside, run classes, play all over camp in our free time, and enjoy the great Northwoods. But rainy days meant something different, yet every bit as fun. Rainy days at an all-boys camp meant jumping in puddles to see who could make the biggest splash, tackling each other in the mud, or better yet, sumo mud wrestling (so much fun!), and then, of course, "showering" in the rain and seeing who could get their hair the foamiest with the shampoo. On rainy days, our creativity was challenged and I was always impressed as the counselors and campers rose to the occasion, every time. The Rec Hall would be transformed into a kind of casino, with each cabin hosting some kind of game of chance. Rest period became a time to write and rehearse cabin skits to perform in the afternoon for the rest of the camp. In the cabins, no matter the age of the boys, elaborate blanket forts would be constructed and sometimes evaluated by a panel of judges that would come around, cabin to cabin. The kitchen would be ready to change the menu at a moment's notice, switching dinner to a hearty serving of warm beef stew on the cold, wet day. And the rainy weather usually meant an extra movie night – an unexpected break from the busy schedule and a chance to get into warm pajamas and run across the wet Quad with a pillow and blanket in hand. These stormy days would end with one of my favorite memories of camp. The youngest boys would squeeze in beside, lean on, and cuddle next to the older boys. And these teen boys understood their role at camp, and on rainy nights, they embraced their role as nurturing "big brothers" for the younger campers. Bob was right, as he always was – a truly beautiful day at Red Arrow.

Reflecting on Your Story

- ♦ When you hear about or experience a person like Bob Krohn, do you admire their positivity, are you skeptical of their outlook, or do you find their enthusiasm annoying? (It's OK, be honest.)
- ♦ What does a "beautiful day" at home and/or at school look like to you?
- ♦ Do you believe that a gray, rainy day can still hold beauty? Explain.
- ♦ How do you or can you contribute beauty to someone else's stormy day?

Exploring Our "WHY"

WWBD

What Would Bob Do? Not a bad question to ask at the start of each new day. Bob's wife, Sue, was kind enough to share her insight into who Bob was and how he lived each day, both in camp and in their lives outside of camp.

Bob and I were married for 51 years and ran Red Arrow together for 45 years. Bob was just a happy person, always upbeat! He loved people and loved to share himself with them. His energy and positive attitude became infectious to hundreds of people at RAC through the years, whether it was in his tennis classes, inspirational chapel talks, or just his smile and greeting for everyone he met in the Quad.

Bob was 60 years old when we left the Chicago area and moved to a small town in Colorado. He was in his element there, as his sunshine attitude and outgoing nature made him popular wherever he went. A 30-minute trip to the post office or the grocery store would take him two hours because he had to stop and chat with everyone. He knew every clerk in the grocery store by name.

Bob just had this rosy outlook on life and few things ever really bothered him. Being his wife and living with Bob was not always easy, however. There were times when concerns had to be addressed, of course, especially when you run a business together. We both called me the "designated worrier." We often joked about it, but I was always confident that Bob's positive attitude would carry us through any difficult situation which arose. He was truly a wonderful person to have as a husband and best friend.

Marriage, like camp, like life, requires the intentional choice of enthusiasm every day, even when "difficult situations" and stormy weather arise. Right? But why? Why did Bob value a smile, an enthusiastic greeting, and a positive outlook so much? Why did he enthusiastically talk to strangers, learn cashiers' names, and balance Sue's worries with his optimism? Well, I don't know if Bob knew the research, but I am sure he experienced it out in Colorado, in his fifty-one-year marriage, and as he led camp well into his seventies: A happy disposition leads to a healthier life. The Mayo Clinic and Johns Hopkins Medicine have done research that reveals the power of positive thinking. Dr. Lisa Yanek and colleagues at Johns Hopkins discovered that people with a family history of heart disease who also had a positive outlook on life were one-third less likely to have a heart attack than those with a more negative outlook (Yanek et al., 2013). Researchers at the Mayo Clinic also explored the effects of positive thinking on health and found that optimistic people have an increased life span, lower rates of depression, lower levels of distress, greater resistance to the common cold, and better psychological and physical well-being (Mayo Clinic, 2020). Like the research from Johns Hopkins, the Mayo Clinic doctors also discovered evidence that a positive outlook leads to better cardiovascular health and reduced risk of death from cardiovascular disease. I am no doctor, but seeing Bob and Sue head out for a bike ride in their seventies is certainly compelling evidence that his positive attitude kept him happy and healthy.

Habits of Positivity

We probably aren't too worried about students' cardiovascular health as they come into our classroom. Yet research shows that the habits they create today will have lifelong benefits. So, teachers and parents, an enthusiastic attitude is good for you and your health, but in developing positivity in your own lives, you are also modeling it for your children and students.

Dr. Barbara Fredrickson, a psychology researcher at the University of North Carolina, offers remarkable insights on the habit-forming power of positive thinking and its impact on one's health and skill development in her book *Positivity*. Through her studies, it is revealed that when a person is experiencing positive emotions like enthusiasm, joy, and love, they will see more possibilities in their life. Her findings are among the first to demonstrate the impact of positivity in broadening one's sense of opportunity and opening one's mind up to solution-oriented possibilities. A person who is enthusiastically open to new possibilities, her research shows, will then create skill-based habits. That is to say, positive thoughts can enhance one's ability to build skills and develop habits needed for success throughout one's life. Dr. Fredrickson refers to this as the "broaden-and-build" theory, as positive emotions broaden one's sense of possibilities, which then allows them to build new skills and valuable habits. So enthusiasm offers more than just "feeling happy" – developing habits of positivity can lead to real-life "success." We see this with Bob. He did not simply wake up one morning and decide every day from that point forward would be beautiful. Rather, throughout his life, he created habits of positivity that kept him open to experiences which built his confidence in the beauty of every day. This confidence in "beauty" improved his relationships, strengthened his problem-solving, and enabled him to be a strong leader, even in the midst of ugly, dark days.

Dr. Fredrickson writes about positivity creating an "upward spiral" that occurs with enthusiastic people: Happiness leads to the development of new skills, those skills lead to new success, which results in more happiness, and the process repeats itself. In other words, happiness, joy, and enthusiasm are both precursors to success and the products of it. Dr. Fredrickson's "broaden-and-build" research proves what Bob knew through his experiences – that enthusiasm is essential to building the habits that allow for happiness and success throughout one's life (Fredrickson, 2009).

I'm No Bob Krohn

Maintaining a "Yes I Can" attitude throughout one's life and building habits of positivity are no easy tasks, and I am not ashamed to admit that sometimes I fail. I get down on myself and I fall into patterns of negativity: complaining, blaming, avoiding, and shaming. Of course, there are times when life is miserable, plain and simple. There are times when our students have major obstacles to overcome. Choosing to make the most of a rainy day is much different than needing to wake up and confront serious realities of grief, depression, anxiety, or trauma. Please hear me – there are certainly times in which the healthiest feelings for you or your students to embrace are your sadness, worry, or anger. These emotions are not inherently "bad" and allowing oneself to feel the entire range of our emotions is needed and healthy. And while Bob was an incredibly positive and inspiring man, I am sure that he had dark days, days in which beauty was hard, if not impossible, to see.

Yet, as educators, one of our roles is to model a positive out-look like Bob did – rooted in our experiences, that offers the assurance that every day won't be dark. We know that there can be growth in the midst of struggle, if one can develop a resilient spirit. We will be exploring the Key of Resilience in a later chapter, but there is a connection here to the Key of Enthusiasm. Modeling and nurturing enthusiasm is a small part we can play in helping our young people develop strong mental health and an internalized optimism to see the beauty in every day, even during the inevitable storms of life.

Inspiring Our Students' Stories

- ♦ How might Dr. Fredrickson's "upward spiral" be experienced by the students in your classroom?
- ♦ How can you affirm your students' full range of emotions and still encourage habits of positivity?
- ♦ How does body language influence emotion? What does authentic enthusiasm look like in your classroom?

Unlocking and Empowering Purpose-Driven Enthusiasm

An Infectious Enthusiasm

In her reflection about Bob, Sue refers to his "infectious" positive attitude and how it spread to all he would meet. Enthusiasm is contagious! Perhaps the most fun way that I find to spread this kind of positive energy is through the power of music and the inspiration of dance. We all have experienced it: We're driving in the car and one of our favorite songs comes on the radio and we sing, loud and proud! Or while making dinner, the music in the background seems to fill our body, and before we know it, we're dancing as we set the table. A powerful, yet easy way to inspire enthusiasm is to bring music into your classroom.

Now, in our efforts to empower and include students, you may be tempted to allow them to choose the music – but here is why I think this "power" should stay with the teacher. You see, today, kids only have to listen to the music they want to listen to. Do you remember as a child listening to your parents' music? I sure do. When my dad drove on long family vacations, we listened to "oldies." I was introduced to Frankie Valli and the Four Seasons, Buddy Holly, The Drifters, and Elvis. My mom loved Herman's Hermits and instilled in me my love for Carole

King. My grandparents introduced me to Frank Sinatra, Andy Williams, Bobby Darin, and Dean Martin. And Bob, in our six-hour drive to Chicago to pick up campers at O'Hare airport, introduced me to the great Tony Bennett singing the perfectly titled "Ac-Cent-Tchu-Ate the Positive."

With cell phones and tablets, our students only ever have to experience their style of music. I found, both in my cabin and in my classroom, the joy of introducing kids to a much wider range of music. Through the power of music and dance, we began class with energy and enthusiasm – even the coolest seventh-grade boys and most skeptical eighth-grade girls smiled, laughed, and joined in. Of course, in my Drama class, we listened to amazing showtunes. No one left my middle school Drama program without knowing the words and dance steps to "Seize the Day" from Disney's *Newsies*! But we also listened to boy bands from the late '90s – a lot of *NSYNC (mostly because Justin Timberlake stole my career). I loved introducing kids to Motown, learning the iconic dance steps of The Temptations and The Supremes. We practiced our Elvis hips, our Fred and Ginger swing, a little Billy Ray Cyrus "Achy Breaky Heart" line dance, and the week of the seventh- and eighth-grade dance, we took class time to learn "The Electric Slide," so they all were prepared. These timeless classics offer the students something new and inspired excitement as they never knew what to expect.

No, I Can't...Yet

An easy concept to grasp, but not always the easiest to believe, is the power of one little word – *yet*. "Yes, I Can" might sound great, but if we're being honest, there are times that it's simply not true. Can I go out and run a marathon today? Yes, I – wait, no, I most certainly cannot. Can I play the guitar? No, I can't. Can any of my campers beat me in wrestling? No, they can't – trust me, every summer many of them try and fail. The reality is that there are lots of things we can't do because we don't have the skills, the understanding, or the desire to do them. So part of a "Yes, I Can" attitude is embracing the power of yet – "I Can't, Yet." It also is kind of fun to "annoy" students with a reminder of "yet" every time they say that they "can't" do something – reminds me of obnoxiously correcting "may" when they ask if they "can" go to the bathroom.

In all seriousness, "yet" transforms a negative statement into a statement of possibility that can lead to the "upward spiral" about which Dr. Fredrickson writes. Today, I can't – but with hard work, collaboration with others, and an open, positive attitude, one day I will. Enthusiastic openness leads to skill-building, skill-building leads to success, and success leads to the happiness needed to be enthusiastically open. So begins a journey of becoming someone who can because you believe that you can. "Yes, I Can" – not yet today, maybe not yet tomorrow, but someday you will!

One Small Step…Again and Again

Goals are the stepping stones on the journey from "I Can't, Yet" to "Yes, I Can." I will offer insight into goal-setting more fully as we explore the Key of Effort, but as with all of the Keys of Purpose-Driven Learning, there is an interconnectedness. Choosing enthusiasm requires putting forth the effort to explore, set, and accomplish your goals. Putting forth the effort of turning the problem of "I Can't, Yet" into a solution-oriented question of "How Can I" takes a positive outlook. We all know friends and colleagues who are great at pointing out the problems of any given day. We need to be, and we need to encourage our students to be, solution-oriented, rather than problem-focused. How do we recognize a challenge and work to set goals to solve the issues, rather than fixating on the problems? You see, when your students are part of the solution, they will be motivated to contribute. As they set goals, they will feel a sense of accomplishment in achieving goals. That excitement of accomplishment leads to a desire to set new goals and work toward achieving them – an upward spiraling, habit-forming routine of becoming one's best self.

At camp, the two cabin counselors sit down every week with each individual camper in their cabin. A 2-on-1, as we call them, allows the campers to reflect on the challenges faced and the goals achieved from the previous week. This time gives them the chance to set new goals for the upcoming week and it offers the counselors the opportunity to provide constructive feedback about the challenges, the camper's response, and the action steps for moving forward. An important aspect is that this reflection, goal-setting, and feedback isn't saved for the end of the summer, but is offered each of the seven weeks. The intentionality of these 2-on-1's allows every camper to prepare for the week ahead with an enthusiastic "Yes, I Can" mentality.

In our classrooms, students' self-assessments and teacher feedback should not wait until the end of quarters, semesters, or the school year. Tied to the habits of positive thinking, goal-setting can become a habit that drives enthusiastic effort within your classroom. While starting at the beginning of the school year is ideal, an educator can begin intentional goal-setting at any time. Begin small – a year-long goal often loses enthusiasm and, therefore, momentum. A big "problem" is rarely solved with one big solution. Taking a "problem-focused" goal and breaking it into smaller short-term, "solution-oriented" goals will provide your students with the success needed to build toward larger accomplishments. It also allows you to offer your students authentic praise and celebrate "mini-successes" throughout the process of learning and growth. What are your students going to accomplish today that you can celebrate at the end of class? How can they map out a series of "solution-oriented" goals that will build into achieving a long-term goal by the end of the quarter or semester?

A Play-Filled Journey

Goal-setting always runs the risk of becoming too serious: getting good grades, making the varsity team, earning the lead role, or getting into the "best" college. Achieving goals is certainly an important way to spark enthusiastic motivation in your students. Yet enthusiasm is not just about the excitement of the destination, it is an essential part of the journey. If goals are the stepping stones on our journey, play is the flowers along the path, the lake to jump in, and the trees to climb. Play is the skipping, leaping, and twirling along our journey.

At camp, we do not focus solely on working toward and earning emblems for our kerchiefs. At camp, we play. We play a lot, every day. Of course, we play during our classes, activities, and free time – basketball, tennis, capture-the-flag, kickball – but we play even at unexpected times. In the Mess Hall, we have a number of games that decide who is scraping the plates and cleaning the table at the end of the meal. Heading down to the lake, really heading anywhere with your cabin, can turn into a race. During rest period, many of the campers play: silently trying to figure out their Rubik's Cube or quietly sitting on each other's bed and playing a game of UNO. Even though these are low-energy types of play, there is definitely still a spirit of enthusiasm.

What does play look like in your classroom? Yes, as a Drama teacher, play is an innate aspect of my pedagogy: We sing and dance, we do acting exercises and improvisation games, and we become different characters and create new worlds. But play isn't contained to the stage, to the gym, or to the playground. All children – heck, all people, no matter the age – need opportunities to play. Do you engage in play? Maybe you go to trivia night or play on a bar-league softball team with friends. Perhaps you and your family have a weekly Game Night or season passes to Six Flags theme park. Play is not just for kids and modeling fun is an important way to inspire a lifelong openness to play. The excitement and energy of play can transform any classroom into an enthusiastic learning environment. In seeing your students' smiles, hearing their laughter, and witnessing their enthusiastic engagement, you will experience the truth that Bob embraced: Each and every day can truly be a beautiful day!

References

Fredrickson, B. (2009). *Positivity: Top-Notch Research Reveals the Upward Spiral That Will Change Your Life*. 1st ed. New York: Harmony.

Mayo Clinic. (2020). *How to Stop Negative Self-Talk*. Retrieved 15 March 2020, from www.mayoclinic.org/healthy-lifestyle/stress-management/in-depth/positive-thinking/art-20043950.

Yanek, L., Kral, B., Moy, T., Vaidya, D., Lazo, M., Becker, L., & Becker, D. (2013). Effect of positive well-being on incidence of symptomatic coronary artery disease. *The American Journal Of Cardiology*, 112(8), 1120–1125. https://doi.org/10.1016/j.amjcard.2013.05.055.

5

The Key of Focus: Looking Within, Raising Awareness Beyond

Connecting to My Story

Distracted – the Story of My Life

Ask anyone who knows me, and I am almost certain that all would unanimously agree on the key that is the most challenging for me: Focus. And if I am being honest, it's true, 100%, without a doubt. My ability to focus, as focus is understood by most people, needs some development. My focus, or lack thereof, in writing this book is a perfect example of the challenges I have faced my whole life, the ways I have embraced my limitations, and how, ultimately, I can find success while still developing my skill of focus. Here's how a typical day of writing goes for me, written in the style of my thinking.

I like to wake up and get started right away, so I get my coffee and I get to work. This morning, I am writing up north at the cabin, so I start my day writing on the couch, because it looks out over the beautiful lake. The room is bright with sunshine and it energizes me, so I take a deep breath and begin – wait, is that a deer on the other side of the lake? I get out my binoculars, and even though I have literally seen hundreds of deer in the

DOI: 10.4324/9781003294634-6

Northwoods of Wisconsin, I watch it for thirty minutes. It takes a drink of water from the lake and I take a drink of coffee from my cup. OK, time to focus, so I put away the binoculars and I take out my computer to start writing. You know, it's kind of cold in the cabin – so I'll just get up for a moment to turn up the heat and I wonder what the weather will be like the rest of the day. I quickly look up weather.com just to peek – after all, I am going to take a break later and, if it is nice, I'll go for a run or maybe a bike ride. Ooo, it's gonna get all the way up to 62 degrees – for May in Wisconsin, that's warm! OK, so get to work. Each of my chapters begins with a story. This story is about the resilience of a Red Arrow camper who had taken a hiking trip – who had took a hiking trip? Had taken, had took? Taken? Took? I honestly don't know which is correct. Well, I don't often edit as I write, but I need to look up which is right. Hmmm – do you know what the present perfect tense of a verb is? I didn't, now I do. Present perfect is a verb tense that is used to show that an action has taken place once or many times before now. So one uses have, has, or had and the past tense of the verb. However, there are verbs, like take, which are irregular verbs. Its past tense is took, but in its present perfect form changes to has taken, like ride, rode, and have ridden or write, wrote, and had written. Wait, where was I – oh yeah, writing my chapter about a camper who had taken a hiking trip. I'll get to it in one moment, my coffee is empty and I need another cup. And before I know it the morning is gone and I have yet to write anything of substance for my chapter.

OK – enough with my story of distraction and procrastination. While it is true that even the most focused among us can get off track, I will openly admit that it does not take much to get me off task.

Diagnosed – Not My Whole Story

Since I was little, and long before I was diagnosed with attention deficit hyperactivity disorder (ADHD), I was that student every elementary school teacher has. Usually, a boy – although, it is important to stress, not always – who is usually enthusiastic and fun, but also very energetic and loud. At elementary school age, students with ADHD are still pretty cute – lots of positive energy that simply needs to be directed and redirected to the task at hand.

At my small parochial grade school, my class was a "big" class with a total of twenty-two students. We were divided into one full class and one split class – so in fifth and sixth grade, I had the same teacher and she was awesome! First, one of her sons was in my class and we were friends, so she knew me outside of school – and I'm pretty sure she liked me. Second, she understood my needs and offered me constructive ways to be out of my seat. She was the first teacher and only teacher I had in grade school who utilized what is now called "flexible seating:" bean bags in the back of the room that she would let students sit in when reading. She also had little jobs for me to do whenever I got antsy. Although, as I look back, I think that some of her "jobs" may have simply been to get my distracting behavior out of the classroom and redirected to a different task. My teacher would give me notes that "needed" to be delivered to teachers in other classrooms or to the office. I am sure the notes said, "Adam was annoying me and I needed a break," but delivering the notes made me feel useful and important in the class. But it wasn't just cool beanbags and note-delivery, she also encouraged me to use my artistic talents and allowed me to decorate the big windows of our classroom. When I needed a break from my school work, I could turn to my creative tasks. With my creativity and some construction papers, I made a scene of autumn leaves that had all the names of my classmates on them, I created a winter wonderland with penguins and snowflakes, and in the spring, I made flowers, bees, and butterflies. Long before it was an educational trend, I had a teacher for two years who took a student-centered approach in her teaching that helped me focus and find success in my learning.

Defined – Living Into and Moving Beyond My Label

I wish experiences like my fifth- and sixth-grade classroom continued throughout my formal education, but unfortunately they did not. They didn't even survive until the following years of grade school, as I entered into seventh and eighth grade. With an attitude of "preparing the students for high school," these teachers' strategies took a dramatic turn toward discipline, rigor, and control. ADHD in teens is treated much differently than in young children. My inability to sit still was seen as a problem that needed to be fixed. My need to talk and connect with classmates was seen as disrespectful. Even though I still got my work done and earned good grades, I was viewed as a "problem" student who needed to be dealt with. I can remember having to stay in during recess to sit at my desk and write out the same sentences a hundred times: "Talking in class is disruptive and disrespectful" or "My behavior is a reflection of who I am." Let me assure any teacher who believes this method of "teaching" holds value – it does not. I did not like my teachers. I did not like school. Because of strong parental support, I managed to be academically successful, but I did not like learning. I did not feel a sense of belonging in my classes. I truly believed that there was something wrong with me. I believed that I "should" be able to sit still, keep my mouth shut, and be a "good" student. And since I couldn't, even when I tried, I eventually stopped trying.

If I couldn't be compliant, I'd be defiant and I became the class clown. Like so many ADHD teenage students, I sought to control what I could. Since I struggled with self-control, I would control the appearance of my lack of focus. Instead of my outbursts being portrayed as a weakness by the teachers, I would make them intentional and funny in the eyes of my peers, so they became a strength, at least in my perspective. I had the power to make the whole classroom laugh and the power to tick off my teacher. With the bravado of a strong-willed teenage boy, I would make school as unenjoyable for my seventh- and eighth-grade teachers as they made it for me. So, a word of warning, my friends – if you have students who struggle with focus, who may appear to be defiant or disrespectful, instead of blaming and shaming them, take a look at your own methods of teaching and discipline. Consider that your expectations are causing insecurities that are leading to resistance, and perhaps even rebellion.

Differentiate – Empowering a Different Story

It won't surprise you to know that, as a teacher, many of my favorite students over the years have been the ADHD middle school students. As kindred, hyperactive spirits, I find a strong desire to make sure they know they are awesome and have lots to contribute. I think they are hilarious and have found that I am much more patient with them than some of my colleagues. This brings me to my story of Richie. He was everything you think of when you picture a little fifth-grade boy with ADHD: a big smile, messy, uncombed hair, and so much uncontrolled energy. I taught at a school with uniforms and poor Richie would struggle to keep his shirt tucked in, his tie "properly" tied and in place, and he never could keep track of his "third piece:" his blazer, sweater, or fleece. Add to this a little, raspy voice that was always excited for Drama class and you get a pretty good idea of the kind of kid Richie was. As Richie finished his senior year and prepared for college, I had the opportunity to reconnect with him and ask him about his feelings and memories of middle school:

During my years in middle school, I experienced a number of learning environments. One significant memory is the experience I had in Drama. It differed from most of my other classes, as I had the ability to freely express myself, as well as release a lot of pent-up energy. The class was always extremely fun, filled with acting exercises created for the purpose of allowing kids to have fun while working on developing different skills, including creativity, collaboration, and self-expression, just to name a few. I've always been a fairly energetic person, so these classes acted as a release for me. I could get rid of some energy in fun yet productive ways. Many other classes, especially core classes, didn't provide this opportunity for me. I was forced to sit and often silently work on my classwork. I struggled to focus in these classes because of this environment, and it would affect my ability to learn the subject at hand.

I was involved with other after-school activities, which included plays, musicals, stage crew, and Junior Thespians. After-school productions absolutely helped me with focus and to develop self-confidence. Learning and memorizing lines and dances takes focus and commitment. One of my favorite memories is when I got to learn the bottle dance for Fiddler On The Roof. Dancing with a bottle on your head? That takes focus! Drama, alongside my love for soccer, allowed me to get rid of excess energy that would have caused my parents to go insane if I had nowhere to let it out. I've had many amazing memories during my time in middle school and the majority of them are thanks to teachers who had classroom environments like Drama and the after-school plays and musicals.

I am thankful that Richie holds amazing memories from his Drama experience. I too have some pretty great memories of his time in my classroom. In speaking with his parents at conferences for four years, I know that other classrooms were not as supportive and other teachers struggled to affirm this dynamic, if often distracted, young man. I worked with won-derful colleagues and I have respect for them as educators, yet every now and then, we would struggle to find common ground on how "unfocused" students should be "handled." To say that Richie was unfocused, impulsive, and scattered may all be true; however, it certainly did not define the entirety of who Richie was and what he had to offer the class. Richie made people laugh and brought enthusiasm to the class that was contagious. He was positive, tried hard, never gave up, and was always ready to work with anyone else in the class.

In sixth grade, students move from ensemble performances to solo performances. After the opening unit of trust-building, improvisation, and risk-taking, these students begin writing and preparing to perform their Superhero monologues. Now, this can be challenging for many of the students, but in Richie's year, it was particularly challenging for a new student. He did not have the experience from fifth grade to empower him and was very nervous about performing. It came to the point where his parents and the Head of the Middle School wanted him to get a "pass" from having to complete his first performance. As explained in the chapter on the Key of Confidence, I have one absolute expect-ation in Drama class – everyone participates, because everyone participates. There may be some flexibility in how one performs, but in all of my years of teaching, no one was excused from an entire performance. And so this young man was allowed to have his monologue script with him, was only expected to get up in front of the class and read it, and that would be the starting point from which he grew more confident in public speaking. We had built a safe environment for him to take this risk and he got up, read the Superhero monologue he had written, and cried the entire time. When the time came to offer feedback, who was the first to raise his hand? Richie – and he praised the performance. You see, every hero has a tragedy in their life that they must overcome. In this monologue, the superhero's parents die (much like Batman's parents). Richie complimented the believability of the parents' death, because his classmate's crying made it seem so real. The young man smiled at the sincere compliment. From that point forward, this young man continued to grow and in eighth grade signed up for the performance elective because, as he told his parents, "Drama was his favorite class." Now, this isn't a story about the young man's transformation, it is about a defining aspect of Richie's story: his ability to focus on the needs of others. Many of my young actors were often too focused on their own performances to truly watch the performances of their classmates and be able to offer authentic and constructive peer feedback, yet this type of feedback was one of Richie's strengths. He always seemed to offer the perfect words for the situation – not always an easy task.

Yes, of course, as Richie has gotten older, he has needed to develop his inner focus to find academic success. Likewise, throughout my adult life, I have had to learn to buckle down and get focused when absolutely necessary – but it is not a skill that comes easy, nor one that I particularly enjoy developing. Yet, in my efforts to holistically grow into the fullness of who I can become, I must not let a diagnosis, such as ADHD, define who I am or who I can be. As teachers, we cannot allow such labels to define how we see our students or how our students see themselves. Let us focus on the whole child, as we explore, learn, and grow together.

Reflecting on Your Story

- ♦ As a child, how would you describe your ability to focus, to stay on task, and to get work done? As an adult, is it the same or is it different?
- ♦ How do you define focus? What does it look like in your life? In your classroom? In your expectations of your students?
- ♦ What is the benefit of allowing yourself to be distracted?
- ♦ In your experience, how does focus connect to learning? To your relationships? To your understanding of the world?

Exploring Our "WHY"

In his book *FOCUS: The Hidden Driver of Excellence*, Dr. Daniel Goleman explores three different "varieties" of focus essential in helping "us find a balance where we can be both happy and productive." Wouldn't it be great to have focused, happy, and productive students! His writings about inner, other, and outer focus are rooted in the work he has done as co-founder of the Collaborative for Academic, Social, and Emotional Learning (CASEL) at the Yale Child Studies Center and now at the University of Illinois in Chicago. Goleman writes, "A leader tuned out of his internal world will be rudderless; one blind to the world of others will be clueless; those indifferent to the larger systems within which they operate will be blindsided." As we explore why the Key of Focus is important in unlocking and empowering our students' passion for learning, we must venture beyond our own singular perspective in order to discover a deeper and more complex understanding of this skill. Yet, as we explore, I believe that there will be a common agreement on Goleman's expanded understanding of focus: As teachers, we embody all three variations.

In his book, Goleman shares a story about a department store security guard mindful of his own self in any given moment, able to focus on specific details of individual shoppers, while maintaining an awareness of the whole store as he patrols. As teachers, most of us have developed this "triple" focus. We are aware of our own feelings and how they may affect our interactions with our students. We can help an individual student while maintaining an awareness of the entire class. We understand systems that are in play – the change of schedule because of an assembly, how we can speak to this student differently than that one, whose parents are going to call if they don't "get their way," how to demonstrate your classroom management style when an administrator unexpectedly walks into the room. Inner, others, outer – experienced teachers tend to be masters of transitioning between these types of focus and often maintain all three types of focus at once.

Inner Focused

Inner focus is what I believe most teachers think of when defining what focus looks like in their classroom. Inner focus is often quiet, if not silent. It embraces stillness, self-control, and calm. It is personal, internal, and reflective. A focus on self is key in one's development: self-awareness, self-motivation, self-regulation, and self-modification. How do we help students discover what inspires them and what distracts them? What are they passionate about and what drives their desire to learn and grow? As we give agency to our students in their learning process, we must nurture inner focus for the awareness needed for effective self-assessment. What are their strengths and challenges? What is helping them achieve their goals? What thoughts, words, or actions are limiting their success? Finally, inner focus empowers self-modification. What needs to change and how do we go about effectively creating and sustaining that change?

Inner focus is not just a struggle for your ADHD students. Yes, hyperactivity and impulse control make this type of focus challenging for those with ADHD, but most of our students need work on developing inner focus. Many of them may have learned to compliantly sit still and be quiet, but that doesn't mean they are actively focused. Nor does talking or movement automatically mean a lack of inner focus. I need to move and I have discovered stronger inner focus as I run – my body is moving, but my breath is even and intentional, and my mind is calm and focused. When I am deep in thought, I speak to myself – there is something about speaking my thoughts aloud that centers me. Inner focus is about oneself – each of us and each of our students are wonderfully unique.

Other Focused

We all know people who have strong inner focus. Sometimes these people are so focused on themselves, they are unaware of those around them. I have had students so focused on their own learning that they unintentionally say or do hurtful things to their classmates, such as refusing to work with someone who struggles academically or insisting that they would rather work alone than in a group of their peers. Goldman warns of the dangers of being solely inner focused on oneself and one's goals. "Single-pointed fixation on a goal morphs into overachievement when the category of 'distractions' expands to include other people's valid concerns, their smart ideas, and their crucial information." If we establish an "A at all cost" learning environment and label a child a distraction, then the other students will marginalize them for the sake of the grade.

Collaboration requires other focus. We know that the key to learning is relationships developed in a safe and supportive environment where students are empowered with a sense of belonging. Healthy, strong, and dependable relationships take intentional development of our other focus: compassion, selflessness, understanding, and inclusion. This is the type of focus at which Richie thrived. Yes, he struggled with inner focus, but his empathy for his classmates demonstrated a strong focus on the needs and well-being of others. We'll dig deeper into other focus as we explore the Key of Empathy, but for now I want to emphasize it as equally as important as inner focus.

Outer Focused

Inner focus is about oneself. Other focus is about our relationships. Outer focus explores our awareness of the "big picture" – the systems that regulate our world. In the world of our schools, they are systems that seek to regulate when, how, and what we learn. Students with strong outer focus are aware of how much time is left when taking their standardized tests or needing to clean up their workstation. They are students who understand that taking a two-week summer class opens their schedule for an extra Arts elective for the entire semester. These students know how to "play the game of school" because they are aware of the systems at play.

Developing the skill of outer focus is essential as our students journey beyond our classrooms and encounter systems of power that influence their lives and the lives of others. As Goleman describes it, they are "the complex systems that define and constrain our world." It calls for a "panoramic awareness" that "helps us grasp the workings of an organization, an economy, or the global processes that support life on this planet" (Goleman, 2013).

Inspiring Our Students' Stories

- ♦ In your opinion, is ADHD truly a "disorder"? How might it be viewed as simply a different way of learning, communicating, or engaging the world?
- ♦ Think of a student or two in your class who has ADHD. How would you describe them to another teacher? What are their challenges? What are their strengths?
- ♦ Which of the three types of focus do you emphasize the most with your students? How can you explore the importance of the other two with your students?
- ♦ Do you treat quiet students who sit still in your class differently than louder students who may move around a lot? Why, and is different treatment needed and/or beneficial?

Unlocking and Empowering Purpose-Driven Focus

Just Breathe

It sounds simple, and it really is, yet we forget about it and often don't utilize its power – the power of breathing. Inner focused during a test – breathe. As a student is trying to remain other focused in a challenging group – encourage a breath. As a student prepares to talk to a teacher about an unfair system of grading – a breath can offer strength. When emotions start to swell and threaten to overwhelm – pause and breathe. Our breath is the very essence of life and too often it is neglected. The first classroom takeaway of this chapter is easy, if we can make it an intentional strategy: Teachers and students must remember to breathe. Yes, yes – everyone breathes. It's part of how we stay alive, but the power of breathing with purpose can be harnessed in our students' learning.

At the start of class, have your students take a few deep breaths. If your students move from class to class, as most middle school and high school students do, your students will benefit from taking a moment to center themselves. Running from class to class with only minutes before they're late, the social drama that manages to occur in those few precious minutes, and the need to shift focus from their last class to your class all require an intentional moment. Known as "box breathing" – have students inhale as you slowly count up to four, have them hold the breath, then have them exhale as you slowly count back to one. A couple of mindful breaths can begin a class with a sense of intentionality and focus. It may seem cheesy when it is new, but I promise, it will be a rare moment in your students' day when they can just breathe.

But mindful breathing does not just have to occur at the start of class. Before a test or a presentation for which they may be nervous is a great time to take a few breaths. In my Drama classroom, my students take a mindful breath every time they stand to address the class. Remember that in my confidence-centered classroom, the students are expected to stand when asking a question, offering an answer, or sharing their thoughts. They stand, take a breath, and then speak. This breath focuses them and allows them to speak with more intentional thought. The breath is key – they breathe in confidence and exhale doubt, then my students share their voice with the class.

Self-Regulation

We need to shift our thinking and move from traditional strategies that falsely equate stillness and silence with focused learning. Setting these expectations lead to disciplinary actions against students who simply focus differently than the traditional method allows. Now, I am not suggesting that students be allowed to move and speak whenever and however they want; rather, I am encouraging you to teach self-regulation. If a student needs to speak or move, it is not the end of the world. But when and how one speaks and moves requires strong outer focus – a focus on what is happening at that moment in the class. Outer focus allows a student to do what they need to do to be successful without taking away from others' learning or disrupting the "system" of the classroom. If they need to move to a standing desk at the back of the room, so be it – move without becoming the attention of the class. If a student needs to speak, find a moment to ask a question or share a thought without interrupting. Students with impulse control issues and hyperactive tendencies will struggle, but the response does not need to be shameful and disciplinary. It can be a self-regulatory question: "Is now a constructive time to move and/or speak?" "I need you in your seat, can you please wait to move until I am done?" "I am going to pause what you are saying. Did you notice another student was speaking?" In order to be inner focused, students do not need to be silent and still, but they do need to be empowered to do what they need to do to learn best. They also need to develop their outer focus, aware that they are not taking away from the classroom learning environment.

Procrastinate With a Purpose

I love the book *The Art of Procrastination: A Guide to Effective Dawdling, Lollygagging, and Postponing* by John Perry. In the book, the author keenly points out that "Anyone can do any amount of work, provided it isn't the work he is supposed to be doing at that moment" (Perry, 2012). I know, I know – this observation might be a little self-serving, but I have found that it is certainly true. I would like to say that it was an essential strategy in my classroom, but the truth is, I discovered it in the writing of this book. My first goal, of course, was to try and avoid distractions – but I am very distractable. When I found myself distracted, I sought to distract myself with something that held the possibility of adding value to the work of completing my book. I have come to call this strategy Purpose-Driven Procrastination (PDP) (gotta stay "on brand," right?). When I was not focused enough to sit at my computer and write, I read books that addressed the social-emotional learning (SEL) skills about which I was trying to write. I watched TED Talks and read blogs about these skills or related topics. I participated in Twitter chats and sought to find ways to include the topic of SEL in my responses. I took the advice of Carrie Baughcum, author of *My Pencil Made Me Do It*, and doodled my ideas for the Keys of Purpose-Driven Learning in my sketchbook (Baughcum, 2019). Was I writing my book? Nope – but through PDP, I was exploring the topic of my book in creative and outside-the-box ways that truly led to more inspired and motivated writing when I finally sat down to write.

How can PDP be encouraged in our classrooms, with our students? As we seek to give students autonomy and allow them to be self-directed, I would suggest offering PDP as a tactic for the unfocused. Instead of giving up or simply plowing ahead without motivation, perhaps procrastination with a purpose might inspire a higher quality of creative work.

Team-Building

Don't roll your eyes – I know that team-building may not be your favorite thing to do in class, but it is so important. Developmentally, children and teens are focused on themselves. It is completely natural and developing strong other focus is not easy. Yet, if we want young people to grow into compassionate and empathic adults, they need to be taught how to focus on others. The truth, which you may not like to hear, is that team-building is not just a first day of school activity. It needs to be a regular strategy for your classroom. May I suggest Team-Building Tuesdays! Take a break from the academic content to intentionally develop your students' awareness and concern for others. I am not going to offer any specific activity because a quick internet search can offer you suggestions, directions, and even videos of team-building exercises for any age in any class. Don't let the singular goal of content-knowledge achievement cause you to view team-building as a "distraction" to learning. I promise that it will strengthen the overall learning experience within your classroom.

Deepening Service

Does your school require your students to complete "service hours?" Does your grade level participate in some kind of community service throughout the year: a river clean-up, visiting a senior center, playing basketball with children who have disabilities? I applaud schools that put an emphasis on service to others. Yet I want to encourage these schools, and all schools, to not just be other focused on their service projects, but to explore how developing an outer focus through service might be experienced. Going to a soup kitchen to help feed the hungry allows our students to focus on the needs of others, but exploring why hunger is an issue in a world that grows enough food to feed everyone can lead students to focus on the systems that help and/or hinder food availability and distribution. Encouraging your students to participate in a Martin Luther King Jr. Day march might help them focus on the needs of people of color, but exploring the systems of racism and white privilege that are perpetuated within our society can empower students to confront these systems in their pursuit to create a better world for *all* people. I encourage schools to emphasize advocacy along with their direct service. We can guide our students from inner focus, to other focus, to outer focus, and back again – transitioning between this triple focus to better themselves, help others, and change the world.

References

Baughcum, C. (2019). *My Pencil Made Me Do It: A Guide to Sketchnoting*. Hanover: Proving Press.

Goleman, D. (2013). *Focus: The Hidden Driver of Excellence*. London: Bloomsbury.

Perry, J. (2012). *The Art of Procrastination: A Guide to Effective Dawdling, Lollygagging, and Postponing*. New York: Workman Publishing Company.

6

The Key of Initiative: Building Involvement and Increasing Impact

Connecting to My Story

Get Up and Get Going

Every teacher has a handful of students that they have taught who leave a lasting impact. Over my tenure in the Drama classroom, I have been fortunate to have quite a number of these students – some you are reading about in this book, some you will hear about in my presentations, and others remain in my heart to be remembered when I need a reminder of why I do what I do. In this chapter, I am going to spend time and share stories about Connor. He was and remains to this day a truly remarkable individual.

When I first became a Drama teacher, Connor was in seventh grade. He was outgoing, funny, and very talented. He was fantastic in helping to develop and then perform in his seventh grade One-Act play in front of the entire middle school. He was a lead in the fall production of *The Lion, the Witch, and the Wardrobe* and a supporting lead in the spring musical, creating a hilarious version of the Mayor of Whoville in our production of *Seussical the Musical*. The following year, Connor continued to shine both

DOI: 10.4324/9781003294634-7

in and out of the classroom, taking both semesters of eighth-grade Theatre Performance, starring as detective "buffoon" Max Smart in *Get Smart*, and demonstrating his immense talent as Professor Harold Hill in a program-defining production of *The Music Man*. Seriously, not to overstate Connor's abilities, but in our first two years working together, he demonstrated his passion for and talent in theatre – a truly incredible young man who continues to take the initiative to reach his goals and follow his dreams.

I am a New York actor – well, I am on a journey to become a New York actor. My theatre journey started in middle school as I discovered and began to develop my skills. I continued to pursue this passion in high school through our school plays and musicals, as well as during Saturday advanced acting classes with Mr. Moreno and Higher Expectations Theatre. After high school, I attended and graduated from a Big Ten school, majored in Theatre and Economics, and jumped feet-first into fame and fortune on the Broadway stage. I'm only kidding; I moved to New York without a job or apartment. I stayed with friends, slept on couches, lived out of two suitcases for eight months as I ran around the city to and from auditions. I worked in Ramen shops, night clubs, and freelanced as an electrician in non-union theatre houses. I have a dream, a plan, goals. But I was never going to find out what lay ahead on my journey simply by dreaming of the Big Apple and the big acting career I desired. I needed to take the initiative to move forward on my journey. A small-town Midwestern boy wasn't going to readily jump feet-first into America's largest city with the stiffest competition for performers anywhere without an inner spark, without something that said, "Hey, this will be worth it." I had to decide to pick up roots, pack the bags, and move to the unknown. Once I arrived – I had to take the initiative to make connections, make opportunities, and make ends meet. The acting roles, the big parts, the training, and the opportunities weren't going to offer themselves unasked on my doorstep.

Did it work? Well, I don't know yet. In the scope of a successful life, I'd say I have hopes for a resounding yes. It's exciting for me because I still have the initiative to keep going. The hustle is still burning. I've cobbled a living outside of a cubicle and normal business hours in the entertainment industry which I love. I've met some incredible people in theatre, film, comedy, design, and many other fields. Perhaps the most surprising of all is that through leaky apartments, rat traps, and garbage piled high on trash day, this small-town boy found a home among it all. The thing about taking the initiative toward your dreams is it can be a rolling rock down a hill picking up speed if you're brave enough to take action. By all means, plan for bumps along the way, but if all you do is dream, plan, and set goals without taking action, you'll never pick up the momentum to go very far.

The world is full of people whispering "settle, settle, settle." They might not understand your goals or dreams. They want you to get a family or a real job or a stable income. But as soon as you get moving in the right direction, initiative gets you up on your feet at sunrise and can keep you going right until bed – working, not waiting, for what you want. As you begin to find glimpses of success, you know you can achieve your dreams. So I continue to dream big – it is impossible to settle for anything less.

Initiative Out of Necessity

"Sorry, your Arts elective doesn't fit into your schedule. Please, choose another." There is – and I think I can speak for all Arts educators when I say this – nothing more frustrating than losing passionate Arts students to scheduling conflicts. At my K12 independent school, all fifth- to eighth-grade students are required to take Drama, Art, and a Music course (Band, Choir, or Orchestra). In high school, these Arts courses become electives. However, just because a student wants to continue following their Arts passion, doesn't mean the class fits into their "academic" schedule. That's right – after four years of deeply engaging the Arts, some students have to take a semester (or whole year) "off" because their Math, Science, English, or History classes conflict with the limited Arts courses offered. Do you know how hard it is to reignite our students' passion after a year away – and that's only if they decide to come back and not fill their elective "spot" with yet another AP course? It's a sensitive issue that many Arts teachers face every year. Oooo – deep breath, end of rant, get to the point. I share this with you because it is in this reality that taking the initiative became a powerful skill for me as a Drama teacher and for my Drama students.

As Connor transitioned from my middle school program into high school at our K12 school, he knew his passion and sought to pursue his theatrical dreams. As he planned for Upper School, he received the disappointing (but all too common) news that the high school acting elective "did not fit into his schedule." He was encouraged to take a two-week summer "Public-Speaking" course to fulfill his Arts credit. That's right – the star of the middle school stage in eighth grade, the recipient of the "Thespian of the Year" award in our Junior Thespian Troupe was told that his passion simply did not fit into the school's "rigorous" academic schedule. He was understandably frustrated, as were his parents. His mother had been my lead Drama parent volunteer the year before and they came to me to see if I could help get Connor into the acting elective. Now, as a middle school Drama teacher heading into only my third year of teaching, it should come as no surprise that my requests for special consideration for Connor fell on deaf ears.

Higher Expectations Theatre

As Connor and his family considered other options for high school, I felt a need to offer him a way to stay at our school and follow his passion. So, I created a theatre company. OK, to call it a company when we first began might be a bit of a stretch, but it was an intentional alternative to what the school offered during the week. I rented the school's theatre and invited eighth graders and high schoolers who were interested and willing to commit to an eight-week Advanced Acting workshop the opportunity to continue the theatre training they began in my middle school program. Twelve students, including Connor, registered for the first workshop – and from there, Higher Expectations Theatre (HET) grew.

I offered an eight-week workshop in the fall, winter, and spring. We studied acting techniques, strengthened improvisation skills, and worked on audition materials for their acting portfolios. The following year, I offered a third- and fourth-grade Saturday morning musical workshop before the advanced acting class. These elementary students would rehearse for a full production of a Disney Kids show. Simple sets, fun costumes, challenging choreography, and beginning performance techniques were taught, and at the end of the eight weeks, the students would perform for their parents. Well, as the years progressed, they performed for their parents, other family members, and an ever-growing audience from the community. Taking the initiative to support Connor's passion developed into an opportunity to ignite the passion of the third- and fourth-grade students before they entered my middle school program. It also gave Connor the opportunity to take the initiative to be the student director of this production and gain a different theatrical perspective. And let me tell you, Mr. Connor, as the little kids called him, was a joy to watch as he taught these budding thespians the art of theatre performance.

I am so proud of the hard work and commitment Connor continues to demonstrate in his life as he pursues a career in theatre. When we take the initiative, our actions certainly have an impact on our own lives. Yet, equally as true – when we take the initiative, our actions can have an impact on the lives of those around us and within our community. Connor's drive will lead to success, I have no doubt of it. Connor's drive also impacts and inspires others including me – as he shows us all what it means to live a Purpose-Driven life.

Reflecting on Your Story

- ◆ Would you consider yourself to be a driven person, a person who takes the initiative to accomplish things or get things done? Why or why not?
- ◆ What are the areas in your life in which you are most motivated to take the initiative?
- ◆ In what areas of your life do you make excuses in order to not take action, move forward, grow, or achieve?
- ◆ Do you have a student or students like Connor, who have discovered a passion in your class and pursued it beyond their time with you?

Exploring Our "WHY"

Inspiring Our Initiative

Why do people take initiative? I certainly did not need to add more work to my plate when deciding to create HET. I was already a full-time Drama teacher with play and musical responsibilities. In the same breath, if starting a theatre company was an interest of mine, I could have done the work to create HET at any time. Yet it wasn't until I knew the impact it could have in Connor's life and the lives of my middle school students heading into high school that I took the initiative to create it. Once created, I continued to take the initiative to invest my time and energy, because the impact continued to grow. In creating a meaningful theatrical experience, there was a huge impact on my Drama program, as I worked with children before they entered middle school and continued with them into high school, even after they left my program. I also saw the impact HET had on the growth of my students as they were able to engage in meaningful theatrical experiences from third to twelfth grade.

Circle of Impact

In his book *Circle of Impact: Taking Personal Initiative to Ignite Change*, Dr. Ed Brenegar speaks to the inspiration I experienced in my theatre program – knowing one's efforts will have a meaningful impact will inspire greater personal initiative. Beginning with a clear purpose that others can understand and buy into, including those inspired by your purpose in the challenging work that needs to take place, and supporting a flexible structure that adapts to inevitable obstacles along the way will help teachers ignite their students' personal initiative.

Clarity of Purpose

Dr. Brenegar and I share a similar passion – getting folks to clearly articulate their purpose. Every school has a mission statement – do your students know the mission, the ideals which define its purpose? Is the mission clear and intentional or is it simply filled with educational buzzwords touted on the website? How is the mission put to use every day for the betterment of the community? That is to say – what tangible impact does your school's mission have on the daily life of your students?

Beyond the mission and guiding principles of our school, I believe that every educator must have a clear mission for their classroom. As spoken about in the opening chapter and supported in Brenegar's research, personal initiative begins with an awareness and understanding of purpose – a purpose that clearly articulates a meaningful impact. Honestly, it is why I wrote this book – so that Purpose-Driven Learning (PDL) is not simply a meaningless "theme" for the school year. It is my hope that administrators, teachers, parents, and students can explore the language of true belonging, holistic learning, and authentic assessment, in order to intentionally take the initiative in the purpose of their school community.

In my Drama classroom, we sought to discover, develop, and demonstrate our innate greatness within our classroom, upon the stage, and beyond our school. I invited students to explore how they would define "their innate greatness," how it might impact their lives, and how it will help to make the world a better place. My purpose is to have a lasting impact in my students' lives. My students understood that their purpose was to have a meaningful impact in the world.

Trusting Relationships

Relationships, relationships, relationships – I've said, now Dr. Brenegar is saying, and, I promise, the more books on social-emotional learning you read, everyone is saying it. It should come as no surprise that in exploring how to ignite initiative, Dr. Brenegar emphasizes the need for trusting relationships (Brenegar, 2018). As teachers, we know this. In creating Higher Expectations Theatre, I was increasing my efforts and energy with my students in order to intentionally extend my opportunity to be in relationship with them and journey with them in their development. Because of this relationship of trust, I knew that, as I challenged them, they would take the initiative to put forth their best effort, complete the work that needed to be done, help make the class and cast a stronger ensemble, and confidently share their passion and skills up on stage in front of a cheering audience. Because of our trusting relationships, my students knew that if they engaged with me in their learning journey, they would achieve things beyond what they ever thought possible. They could experience greatness and they would be celebrated for their efforts.

Structural Agility

When entering high school, Connor wanted to follow his passion. He wanted to take the initiative to continue to learn the art of theatre, grow in his acting abilities and confidence, and use theatre as a tool to have a meaningful impact in his life. Yet the structure of our school schedule refused to adapt to allow this type of impact. Isn't this a truth of educational structure far too often – that the biggest obstacle to the purpose of schools is the structure of schools and its inability to adapt to students' needs?

The initial structure of my theatre program included my middle school students. Through Higher Expectations Theatre, it adapted and expanded to include younger and older students. The little third and fourth graders were at the start of their learning journey. By the time my students had the opportunity to take Advanced Acting, they fully bought into our purpose, we had established trusting relationships, and they could more fully be included in the process of their learning and growth.

The structure of our classrooms must proactively include students in the process of their learning. It must then be flexible enough to adapt to the needs, the feedback, and the growth of the students. Funny enough, when the Keys of PDL were being identified and developed, adaptability was one of them. Over time, the ability to adapt became a key aspect of resilience and so was no longer a "stand-alone" key, but nevertheless, it is essential in the construct of our class structure and systems.

Personal Initiative

In my classroom, as part of an "exit ticket," I would sometimes ask my students to identify a way that they helped to make class "better" that day. At camp, I would ask the campers in my cabin a similar question every night before turning off the lights – how was camp a better place because you were here today? It is a powerful question that challenges us to consider the impact we have on the communities in which we live. It isn't meant to shame anyone who cannot come up with an answer. Rather, with intentional explanation and effective follow-up discussion, it is meant to encourage intentional action so we have an answer the next time the question is asked. It is also a wonderful way to point out the little things we have done and will do that can have a meaningful impact on the lives of our family and friends.

I encourage you to ask your students – why is our classroom a better place because of your presence in it today? Why is this school, your home, your community, the world a better place because you lived in it today? We can ask such a challenging question because, though many are not aware of their impact, I believe that everyone has an impact on those around them. Every day does not need to be a "Save the World" kind of day – perhaps today their impact was simply making someone smile, a small act of kindness, or offering a word of encouragement to someone who needed it. As teachers, we can help our students become more aware of their impact and empower them to take the initiative to have an even greater impact each and every day.

Inspiring Our Students' Stories

- ♦ Do your students know, understand, and buy into the purpose of your classroom?
- ♦ Why might our students be hesitant to take the initiative in our class? In their own growth and development? In trying to achieve their goals?
- ♦ How can you build trusting relationships with your students to help them explore and discover possible passions in their lives?
- ♦ What is the balance of nurturing our students' dreams and goals versus offering them a healthy dose of reality?

Are we helping them journey toward something ridiculous or achievable? Does it matter?

♦ Is the structure of your classroom a help or hindrance to the initiative of your students? How can the structure of our classrooms adapt to continually offer our students opportunities to take the initiative in their learning journey?

Unlocking and Empowering Purpose-Driven Initiative

Look for the Helpers

From the youngest to the oldest of us, the first step of learning is often imitation – so, as we explore the power of initiative, we must look for role models. I love Mr. Rogers – I mean, who doesn't love Mr. Rogers? He is such a great role model. He was an ever-present voice of assurance, positivity, and joy throughout my childhood. Mr. Rogers always had great advice, and as we explore the Key of Initiative, his words offer a needed perspective for all of us. He shares, "When I was a boy and I would see scary things in the news, my mother would say to me, Look for the helpers. You will always find people who are helping" (PBS, 2012). Beauty, strength, hope can be found, even in the worst of circumstances, by looking for those who take the initiative to help, by looking "for the helpers." They are not always easy to spot, as the work they do is not done for attention or acclaim. They are in the background, doing what needs to get done, having a meaningful, yet often underappreciated impact. "Seeing the good," recognizing those often overlooked, and expressing appreciation for their efforts helps our students build a positive and hope-filled perspective of the world.

However, these "helpers" can offer our students more than hope. They actively help individuals and communities in need. They are taking the initiative to change the world. In our classrooms, we can lift up these helpers as role models – doing more than simply "talking the talk." They are "walking the walk." While bringing in a nationally known guest speaker to a student assembly may only be able to happen once a year, schools can bring in community helpers, like firemen, police officers, first-responders, nurses, and Red Cross volunteers, throughout the year. They are usually willing to speak for free, and your school can even take the initiative to donate the budgeted "speaking fee" to the community organization. Of course, supporting these community "helpers" with our gratitude is also a great way to recognize them, and "Thank You" cards or an appreciation video message can be a creative and meaningful class project. These people are so important. They can become for our school community the very thing we hope to be for our students – confident and compassionate examples of the power of initiative. Mr. Rogers encourages us to look for the helpers and, perhaps, lifting up the helpers within our community can inspire us to be the helpers the world needs, working together and having a lasting impact as we journey together.

Heroic Initiative

In the 2017 movie *Justice League*, Batman has assembled a powerful team of heroes. The Flash, in this movie, is just a teenage boy, and in the midst of his first battle, he is scared. He doesn't think of himself as a hero and is at a loss of how he can help. Batman offers him wisdom that I feel we all can learn from, telling young Flash to use his special power of speed to save just one person.

How many of our students are facing situations they have never faced before, are encountering obstacles they could never dream of, and are being asked to overcome challenges they do not feel equipped to conquer both inside our classes and beyond our school communities? The challenges in their lives are many: the demands of our classrooms, of their families, of their everyday lives. It makes sense that they might be scared – which is a valid feeling when thrust into situations that they feel unprepared to face. Fear can cause us to freeze and fail to take action. It is in these moments that we can empower our students with Batman's words to save just one, take the initiative to do one thing. Of course, we most likely are not asking our students to save people from supervillains, but we can challenge them to do what they can, here and now, to do their best, face challenges, overcome obstacles, learn as they journey, and grow every day. In some ways, we are asking our students to make themselves and our shared world better by taking the *initiative* to act.

Heroic initiative is our superpower! Being brave enough to take the first step, having the courage to speak up and speak out, actively seeking out others to join us on our hero's journey. For that is what we all need to undertake – a journey throughout our lives in which we do not ignore the struggles of others or run away from our own fears, but rather we need to come together to face them. Save one – make one confident decision, one bold choice, one intentional action.

And after our students have taken this first step, what comes next? Well, the Flash asks the same question and I offer Batman's answer. You will know what to do next. Spoiler: The Flash goes back into the fray and saves one more, then another, and another, until he ends up saving every person. No fighting, no battling – his mission was to use his skill and take the initiative to rescue those in danger as the other heroes fought. He didn't set out to save them all, but in rescuing one at a time, he saved the day. Each of our students has a role to play, skills to contribute, and abilities that are needed. What couldn't they accomplish, if they'd only begin – one challenge, one obstacle, one learning opportunity at a time?

Stop and Step Back

It might sound obvious, but before taking the initiative in any situation, we must stop, take a step back, and ask ourselves, "What needs to be done?". Too often we take one of two other options. Sometimes, in our eagerness and passion, we jump right in and begin to seek solutions when, in all actuality, there is no problem to be solved. I often was assigned recess supervision as a Drama teacher, and I cannot tell you how many other teachers wanted to jump in and take the initiative to solve the daily playground "problems" of the impromptu sixth-grade flag football game. Almost every day, the students playing the pick-up game would argue over a certain play, a catch, or a rule. Several teachers felt a need to jump in, offer solutions, and make up more rules to "fix" the problem for future games. Yet every day they would argue. I took a different approach – I did nothing. I did not take the initiative to solve their problem, because it wasn't really a problem. When nothing was done, the students would figure it out on their own. It only took them a couple of recesses to realize that arguing the whole time wasn't as much fun as playing. They would still argue at times, but would reach a resolution pretty quickly without any adult interference.

The other option often taken is to feel that nothing can be done or that the problem is someone else's and therefore nothing is done. As I substitute, I see this option – as a new person in the school, when a problem arises that needs attention, I try to find a person who can address the issue. Yet time and time again I hear, "That's not my problem," and I am directed to someone else. The behavior in the lunchroom is out of control, while a table of teachers simply turns a blind eye and deaf ear. Copier jams – and the user simply leaves it for the next person. The next person comes in and, rather than unjam the copier, they leave and plan to make copies the next day when hopefully it is fixed.

Taking the initiative requires intentionality and awareness. Before jumping in, reflect on what needs to be done. Before walking away, reflect on who is impacted by your indifference. Every problem is not ours to solve, yet problems that do not directly affect us might benefit from our involvement. Stop, step back, and assess what is needed.

Follow Through

Initiative is not just about taking the first step – it requires follow-through until the task is complete. How many of us know people willing to volunteer, jump in, take the initiative, and plan on taking action? Yet these same people fail to actually take action or fully complete the actions they were initially so eager to begin. We will explore the effort needed to have an impact after one takes the initiative as we explore the Key of Effort. For now, I simply want to emphasize that the Key of Initiative is a needed skill and the first step in one's journey, but it certainly is not the only or the last step.

As Connor spoke about earlier in this chapter,

The thing about taking the initiative toward your dreams is it can be a rolling rock down a hill picking up speed if you're brave enough to take action. By all means, plan for bumps along the way, but if all you do is dream, plan, and set goals without taking action, you'll never pick up the momentum to go very far.

Wise words from a remarkable young man. So do not be afraid to hold your students accountable. Do not be offended when your students, with whom you have built relationships, seek to hold you accountable. We all must take the first step, then support one another in continuing to move forward until we have made an impact that will last.

References

Brenegar, E. (2018). *Circle of Impact: Taking Personal Initiative to Ignite Change*. New York: Savio Republic.

PBS. (2012). *Mr. Rogers Post Goes Viral*. PBS News Hour. Retrieved 14 January 2021, from www.pbs.org/newshour/nation/fred-rogers-post-goes-viral.

7

The Key of Creativity: Leveling Up with the Gamification Guru

Connecting to My Story

All Hail the King

"The king is dead." Torin, Remal, Zemar, Aleria, and Tovar – each house within the Realm of Nobles must now compete for control of the throne. Who will accept the challenge? Who will rise up and journey forward on this adventure? Who will seek the greatness to which they are destined? With this dynamic storyline, the sixth graders of Michael Matera's World History classes begin a learning journey that is anything but common within schools today. Through creative play, Michael transforms the experience of his students from being passive recipients of content to active seekers of learning. Engaging in a process known as gamification, Michael takes his content and embeds it into a year-long "game." Students become characters within the world of the game, needing to undergo an adventure to explore, discover, and obtain new levels of learning. Like all engaging video games, his young adventurers move from level to level within the game, from unit to unit within the school year. Along the way, they need to obtain items to help them on their journey,

DOI: 10.4324/9781003294634-8

they achieve badges of honor and power, and they earn experiential points (XP) for their houses. Michael's students also have the opportunity to deepen their learning and earn additional XP for their team by completing optional sidequests and adventure paths. They compete at times, must collaborate at other times, and throughout the game must develop and demonstrate key skills and knowledge. Does this sound like any class you were a part of as a child? No – me neither. Yet in his book *Explore Like a Pirate*, Michael assures all teachers that "gamification is possible in any classroom because creativity is the wind that powers the sails" (Matera, 2015).

Journey of Discovery

As a Drama teacher, I have always considered myself pretty creative and can see the innate creativity of my students thrive within my Arts classroom. However, Michael describes his own exploration and discovery of creativity as a journey. Perhaps one of the qualities I respect most about Michael is his willingness to learn, reflect, and adapt his teaching in his pursuit of having the greatest impact on his students' holistic development.

Throughout my life, I have often struggled with the notion of creativity. I felt like it was something others had and I didn't. I wondered how they were able to get so much of it and I had so little. In my first few years as a teacher, I would ask students to apply creativity to their assignments. Some would creatively connect content in a free-flowing style and make it come to life. It was beautiful. However, it was rare. I took this as some sort of proof. It was evidence of the two sparring groups of the haves and the have nots that would surely continue to struggle for the limited creative capital in our world.

Then, I decided to attack my own scarcity mindset around this topic. I started by challenging myself to be more observant of the world around me. Being observant was the kindling that helped light my creative fires. I could now see ideas everywhere; from a walk in the park to the drive to work. My eyes were open. I could now see the abundance of ideas and the only scarcity was my intentions to bring them to life. Empowered with endless ideas, I set out to create and it was exhilarating.

I started to yearn for more time to create than consume. I read more, I saw more, and I felt more so that I could metaphorically parkour from one new idea to another. Throughout this process I learned more than just ideas, I learned new skills and tools that helped me create in new ways. In my journey, I learned that creativity has a unique property; the more you use it, the more you have of it. This forever changed my view on life and my classroom. I have come a long way since I walked into my first classroom in Italy. Now, as a sixth-grade World History teacher, author of two books, and host of a podcast, YouTube channel, and Hive Summit, I see how being creative is a gift you not only give yourself but also offer the world.

This feeling is one that I want to make sure students tap into and never lose. Creating a highly differentiated classroom that gives endless opportunities for students to apply creativity and level up their skills became my goal. One way this was achieved is with how I approach teaching with game-inspired course design and gamification. My students are constantly asked to create. Daily, I say that we need to fuse content and creativity together. This intersection is where sparks start to fly. From paintings of Rome to replicas of ancient inventions, my students are fully engaged in their learning and the application of creativity. Students shouldn't be the audience for their own learning. It is important that we continue to push our own thinking on where creativity can play a role in our classrooms. The world needs new ideas and our students certainly have just what is needed.

Driven to Have an Impact

Do you know people who get up in the morning and never stop going? At times in my life that has very much been me – up and working out at 6am, so I can be showered and at school by 7:30am. I get coffee and set up my classroom for a day of theatrical arts. I teach an entire day – two fifth-grade classes, two sixth-grade classes, one seventh-grade class, and one eighth-grade class, along with recess duty, lunch table responsibilities, and study hall supervision. The bell for the end of the day rings at 3:15pm and I head down to the theatre for middle school musical rehearsal until 5:30pm. Once the final student is picked up (always late), I rush across town to my own community theatre rehearsal in which I have earned a lead role. From 6:30pm–9:30pm, I am the "student." The director and choreographer work with me as I rehearse my songs, my lines, and my dance steps. Then I head home to spend an hour working on the blocking and choreography for the third- and fourth-grade Saturday morning musical. I go to bed by 11pm, knowing that my morning workout will begin again at 6am. Go, go, go – well, most of the time.

It's not surprising that Michael and I became such strong colleagues and good friends. He is equally as driven – no, he is probably even more driven than I am. He wakes up at 5am every morning because he read in a book that successful people function on six hours of sleep. So, before he leaves for school, he has put in two hours of work on whatever his latest passion project is. He moderates a Twitter chat (#XPlap), has written two books (*Explore Like a Pirate* and *Fully Engaged*), hosts a podcast (Well Played), produces an educational vlog (Finding Joy in the Journey), and founded an immensely successful virtual professional development conference that he hosts every August (Hive Summit). During the global pandemic, while I had trouble getting out of my pajamas each day, Michael not only turned his entire gamified class into a virtual game, he also led online, live-streamed Game Nights (Let's Play) with educators and families all over the country. During this time, he also worked with another innovative educator, John Meehan, to create the emc2learning educational platform – an online community that offers amazing creative play resources and courses that can be used in every classroom. And he creates all these things while teaching full time and being an amazing dad. Yeah – Mr. Matera is crazy driven and his journey of creativity has produced some truly remarkable things.

Play-Filled and Purpose-Driven

The connection that Michael and I share is not just based on being driven. It's a shared passion for being driven for a purpose and inspiring this intentional drive within our students and our school communities. In my words, our purpose is to help others unlock their innate greatness. In his words, our purpose is to empower others to "leave a legacy." Impacting the lives of others and the world around us is a big purpose, so we break it down into steps that we can take along our journey. As teachers, there is no greater impact we can have within our classrooms than to offer our students an affirming space of belonging in which to grow in confidence, to explore their creativity, to collaborate with others, and to discover and share their passion. Michael uses gamification to intentionally have this type of meaningful impact on his students.

Through gamification, Michael emphasizes more than just the skill of creativity in his classroom – since early in the development of Purpose-Driven Learning (PDL), Michael has been committed to intentionally implementing the whole pedagogy within his teaching. Michael writes, "Purpose-Driven Learning gave me a voice with which to lead and inspire my students" (Matera, 2015). He has found that PDL offers a language of learning needed in his non-traditional, gamified classroom. It provides an intentional focus on the very skills he seeks to develop within his young adventurers – nurtures a curious spirit of exploration, empowers confident risk-takers, motivates learners to take the initiative within the game and put forth their best effort, develops dependable teammates within the competition, and, of course, embraces the innate creativity in both his students' play and the learning it produces.

Reflecting on Your Story

- ♦ Do you consider yourself to be a creative person? Do you consider your content area to be a creative subject?
- ♦ How might the journey of Michael's discovery and development of his creativity inspire you?
- ♦ Reflect on moments you have been creative in your teaching – when and in what ways has creativity inspired you as an educator?
- ♦ What obstacles to creativity do you face within your classroom? How might you confront and overcome these obstacles?

Exploring Our "WHY"

An Educational Renaissance

I first met Michael in my second year of teaching when he became the sixth-grade World History teacher at the school where I taught Drama. We quickly became one another's "go-to" colleagues as we shared a passion for non-traditional teaching and creative play. In fact, in those early years, we would meet for an hour before school to set goals and discuss our teaching. We even created an educational manifesto. Over a decade ago, we declared: *"A change needs to take place. It's time for something different – something drastically, holistically, fundamentally different. It's time for a Renaissance. A rebirth. It's time to let the old ways die and nurture to life something new."*

One of us being a History teacher and the other a Drama teacher, it makes sense that we were drawn to the language of a renaissance. The Renaissance was a period in European history marked by a cultural flowering of creativity and creative thinking: distinctive arts, intellectual achievements, and scientific advances. The advent of printing brought about a greater breadth of knowledge and greater access to education for the common people. The period was dubbed by many nations as the "Golden Age" and countries sent ships to all corners of the world to learn about new places, people, and innovations. Numerous scientists, artists, philosophers, poets, and writers rose to great notoriety during the Renaissance. New techniques in painting, music, poetry, and theatre were developed, and scientists pondered the nature of the heavens and put forth theories on the basic workings of the world. European society also changed dramatically as the Renaissance reformed attitudes about government, rights, religion, and wealth. Amazing! I don't know about you, but I definitely think this world is ready for another Renaissance.

People, no matter the era, have an extraordinary amount of creativity. Your students are amazingly creative. *You* have untapped creativity waiting to be discovered and explored. Yet, for our creativity to flourish, certain aspects of our educational strategies have to "die" in order to give light and life to new, more innovative techniques. We need to take a hard look at our teaching practices that are out-of-date and ineffective. We need to be courageous enough to let go of these old ways, in order to fully embrace the potential for something more life-giving. Band-aid fixes and patchwork solutions have failed to build a strong and sustainable educational structure. So let's stop spending time, energy, and money keeping this failed structure on life-support. I say, let it die. Let us believe that together we can build something stronger, more equitable, and more impactful.

Whenever I speak of a need to let old ways die, someone inevitably points out that not all old ways are "bad" – and they are right. However, even if we cling to the positive old, our hands are full and cannot grasp the creative new. Here is what I believe – if there are constructive and effective traditional ways of teaching and learning that we let die along with the destructive and ineffective ways, they will be reborn in the exploration of the new. The powerful truths of learning cannot truly die; rather they are reborn. In fact, a true Renaissance is not only the discovery of progressive innovation; it is the rebirth of the old in creatively new ways. The European Renaissance was not only the birthplace of new artistic and scientific ways of thinking; it was the rebirth of classic understandings of learning. These classic ways were explored and engaged in new ways during the Renaissance. Let this be our mission, our vision, our purpose – an educational Renaissance that brings new life and rebirth within our schools and classrooms, within our hearts and minds.

Right-Brainers Rule

In his book *A Whole New Mind: Why Right-Brainers Will Rule the Future*, Daniel Pink maintains,

> We are moving from an economy and a society built on the logical, linear, computerlike capabilities of the Information Age to an economy and a society built on the inventive, empathic, big-picture capabilities of what's rising in its place, the Conceptual Age.
>
> (Pink, 2005)

Knowing and recalling the infinite amount of information we now have access to is not as important as knowing how to acquire, assess, and apply this information in new and creative ways. Pink made this claim way back in 2005 – and most of us would agree, schools have been very slow to embrace this reality. We are spending valuable class time requiring students to memorize information that they have access to in a matter of seconds on their devices. The analytical assessment and creative application of our content is something we get to only if we have time – and far too often, we don't find the time. Daniel Pink would say that we are out of time and must change now. Schools must move from a focus on left-brained teaching strategies to right-brained learning strategies in which the development of creativity is prioritized. We must help students develop a new, more holistic mind that will be ready for the challenges of a future for which we cannot fully prepare them.

More Than Artistic Expression

As a Drama teacher, it would have been very easy to write a chapter on creativity from the perspective of the arts. Certainly, arts integration – music, theatre, dance, visual arts, design, and writing all are amazing ways to explore the creativity of our students. I cannot emphasize enough the importance of the arts in school and arts integration within every classroom. In fact, one of the amazing aspects which gamification offers within a classroom is the opportunities to express one's learning in artistic ways. Sidequests and adventure paths allow students to offer various artistic projects – Lego builds, drawings, video creation, play-dough models, creative writing. Really, the possibilities are endless.

Yet the creativity embraced through gamification can address so much more than just artistic expression. It can encompass creative problem-solving and solution-seeking as the assigned gamified tasks challenge students to work together, overcome obstacles, and move forward throughout the story that has been created. It encourages a creative perspective of the world – seeing the big picture from various points of view, asking questions that have not been asked, and discovering unique ways different pieces of the puzzle can fit together. If we train students to only see the content of our teaching from our perspective, we will miss out on their unique perspective. And as Michael says, *"The world needs new ideas and our students certainly have just what is needed."* Gamification offers the opportunity for our students to fully engage our content and their learning in new ways that will change our understanding of effective teaching.

Inspiring Our Students' Stories

- ♦ Do you think your students are confident in their innate creativity?
- ♦ What opportunities do your students have to express their creativity and creative problem-solving skills within school? Outside of school?
- ♦ How can you design your teaching in order to more intentionally engage the right side of your students' brains – the creative side?
- ♦ How might gamification and creative play engage your students to help them connect to each other and the content more authentically?

Unlocking and Empowering Purpose-Driven Creativity

Creative Play

OK, so Mr. Matera has been doing this for a really long time. What can we learn from him? How can we use the tenets of gamification to transform our classroom? Gamification takes the mechanics of games and applies them to the pedagogy of learning. What are your favorite aspects of games? Imagination and wonder are inspired. High-stakes challenges are boldly taken. The fun is player-centered and each player can engage the game from multiple entry points. Michael breaks down these mechanics into three categories that I find helpful: theme, team, and task. As we explore how we can ignite creativity within our teaching and our students' learning, let's use these mechanics as a foundation.

Theme – an Adventure Awaits

Both Michael and Daniel Pink agree that the power of story motivates engagement and connection. Create a story in which your students can be active participants. Creating a theme or multiple themes in your teaching can motivate your students and create meaningful connections to your content. Michael uses macro-gamification within his class. He has a year-long theme that is based on a Medieval storyline – castles and nobility, quests and adventures, tournaments and battles. Instead of taking on the entire year, perhaps, you can start smaller and apply micro-gamification in the creation of a theme for a single lesson – western, sci-fi, historical, fantasy, dystopian. You can have your students become characters within this theme: time travelers, pirates, superheroes, or government agents. Connect your content to the theme – reading a graph becomes deciphering a code, a lab experiment becomes a race to find a cure, reading a text becomes a hunt for clues to the next level of the adventure. Everyday, routine activities take on deeper importance: Completing homework is how your superhero students can increase their power, collaboration is the assembling of the Justice League or the Avengers, a simple review for the upcoming test becomes a battle against an evil supervillain.

Like I have emphasized elsewhere in this book, intentional language is key and effective gamification requires this intentionality – test reviews become Boss Battles, exams become Ultimate Challenges, homework becomes Quests. This change in language might seem insignificant, maybe even a little cheesy – but time and time again, educators who have implemented gamification find that themed language changes how the students engage these tasks. Honestly, there is no limit to how dedicated to a theme you can be – a bathroom pass becomes a key to the outhouse, a locker pass becomes a key to transport back in time when the student was at their locker before class, and a pass to the office to see the principal becomes a letter to the queen. Seriously, get parchment paper, wax, and a signet ring, write in old English, and seal every pass: *"Your Royal Highness, this unruly serf has caused considerable tribulation within the House of Moreno, the second period of the fifth day in the month of November. Chastise him to the fullest extent of the law, until it pleases your most just nature. With much respect and admiration, your humble Lord Moreno."*

Chances are, if you are an elementary school or middle school teacher, you have experimented with themes in your lessons before. You hear about the creativity of gamification and, hopefully, want to explore more. High school teachers, some of you may get excited about creating a themed lesson – but for some reason, many folks think that high schoolers won't buy into creative play. Let me tell you, when a space of belonging is created, they will be willing to take the risk of active engagement. Students of all ages – in fact, *all* people want to have fun, want to play – sometimes, fear keeps us from the full experience of freedom offered through in play. Now, it certainly will look different depending on the age, but I promise, a well-thought-out themed lesson *will* be more engaging and have greater buy-in than your forty-five-minute lecture. Adding an engaging theme allows for a sense of being transported beyond the walls of your classroom, into a new world. It is why movies and theatre are so popular – a moment of escape from the ordinary. Creating a themed lesson, unit, or entire curriculum allows your students to engage the content in extraordinary ways.

Team – Gamers Assemble

How are your students going to engage the content? As individuals? As partners? Small groups? Or maybe a specific task requires the entire class to work together. "Team" is simply challenging teachers to be intentional with how their students are collaborating with one another or competing against each other. Both of these styles offer exciting possibilities. Collaboration heightens connections between classmates. Healthy competition motivates greater energy and effort. Both can deepen our students' connection with the content as they engage it in order to achieve something together or to beat out the others for the win. Either way, an intentionality with teams allows for a sense of inclusion – as students become part of something greater than their individual engagement.

Teams can look a number of different ways. Teams can be assembled within classes – small groups that compete against each other within the class period. However, getting creative, teams can also be assembled across class periods. In Michael's sixth grade, students compete within each period and across the periods. In his Greece unit, there are students within each city-state in every class period. For example, the success of the city-states of Sparta or Athens in second period benefits the same city-states in third, fifth, and seventh periods. It is exciting to see students talking about their city-state, the content, and the competition outside of class – during recess and at the lunch table. The connection to one's "team" can also extend beyond the school year, as Michael often has former students stop by his class to see how their House in the Realm of Nobels is doing that year. In fact, Michael invites back alumni to compete during recess for the glory of their House. They also stop by to give inspirational speeches to their House and, at times, offer strategies for upcoming challenges. It is a powerful testament to the connection his students feel to the teams they were on.

Tasks – Literally, the Things You Do

Tasks allow the theme to come to life and give teams their purpose. It is *what* you do in a gamified class with an intentional focus on the *how* and *why* these tasks engage specific gaming mechanics. How does a time limit affect the students' focus when completing this task? Why must they use Lego to build their design instead of simply drawing it on a piece of paper?

I feel a need to clarify the importance of this intentionality within gamification. Gamification is not simply playing games. The task of playing Kahoot or Heads Up 7 Up as a reward on a Fun Friday is not gamification. In gamification, the motivation for engagement isn't a game at the end of the lesson or unit, it is the learning and growth that occurs during the lesson or unit. It is using the knowledge gained to successfully win a Boss Battle. It is the desire to complete a build challenge and articulate the various elements with the structure.

Two tasks I want to discuss are mentioned several times within this chapter: sidequests and adventure paths. These tasks are unique because they offer students a challenge beyond the required work within Michael's classroom. Sidequests are projects that students complete to deepen their understanding of the content. These sidequests are not graded, though a demonstration of knowledge, effort, and creativity will earn students additional XP, badges, and items to use within the game. Adventure paths, like sidequests, are optional. These tasks invite students to choose a more challenging path through the unit. These students know that more will be expected of them, but through the experience, they are told they will gain a greater connection to the content and greater confidence in their resilience. Now, not choosing to complete sidequests and not choosing to undertake the adventure path does not hurt a student's final grade. However, the students quickly realize that if they only engage the required content and avoid challenging tasks, their experience in sixth grade World History will lack the same excitement and engagement as their peers who fully participated in the game. Excitement and engagement in learning are intentional choices they must be willing to make.

Gradeless

We will talk more about what a gradeless classroom can look like in the chapter about self-assessment. However, as we explore how we can develop our students' creativity and creative confidence, I must emphasize how damaging grades are. In my final years as a Drama teacher, I utilized a gradeless model of teaching and saw the creative effort of my students soar, as they were no longer bound by the fear of failure or the sole focus of "getting an A." Similarly, Michael has found great success in moving toward a gradeless classroom, as a focus on self-assessment and student-centered feedback takes priority. His students are willing to give an honest assessment of their engagement, understanding, and growth because they do not fear being shamed, losing points, or failing to achieve a certain grade. The students' creativity thrives throughout his gamified classroom because the goal of his game, the purpose of his classroom, is holistic growth and development.

Find Your Person

Michael is, as Meredith and Christina from Grey's Anatomy would say, "my person." There has been no one more influential in my development as an educator and as a person. I am thankful for the impact in the educational world that we have been able to have together over the years. And even more, I am thankful for the friendship we have created. I hope every teacher can find their person – the person who supports you, challenges you, and journeys with you in your mission to change the world.

References

Matera, M. (2015). *Explore Like a Pirate: Gamification and Game-Inspired Course Design to Engage, Enrich, and Elevate Your Learners.* San Diego: Dave Burgess Consulting, Inc.

Pink, D. (2005). *A Whole New Mind: Why Right-Brainers Will Rule the Future.* New York: Riverhead Books.

8

The Key of Dependability: Showing Up and Doing Your Part

Connecting to My Story

The Art of Athletics

"Ready, break!" The team breaks from the huddle and approaches the line of scrimmage. "Down" – the linemen, running backs, and receivers get prepared for what is to come next. "Set" – the hands of the linemen snap down, the running backs set in the backfield, and the receivers square to the line ready to go. As if part of the play, there is a moment of silence as the team takes a collective breath…inhale, exhale. "Go" – the ball is snapped and a play that has been practiced a hundred times is executed. The quarterback drops back. The linemen set into pass protection. The weak-side guard pulls and heads down the line to pick up the defensive end. The wide receiver runs a deep post to clear the safety on the strong side. The halfback protects the blind side from the blitzing outside linebacker as the quarterback throws a perfect spiral to the tight end open in the flat. The ball is caught and the tight end turns downfield and picks up eleven yards before being taken down by the safety. The team hustles back to the huddle – first and ten, time to do it again.

Football is a beautiful sport. I know, I know – a bunch of guys bashing into each other as a sport seems rather caveman-like. And, without question, the kind of money pro footballers get

DOI: 10.4324/9781003294634-9

paid to play a game is ridiculous. But what can I say – I love the strategy and execution of the game. Like a choreographed dance – the team moves together as one, cohesive unit – each player having a specific series of actions to complete in order for the play to be successful. These actions are timed with the actions of the other players. The plays are practiced and practiced and practiced until each movement is executed with precision. Since fifth grade, I have played quarterback on my teams – a position that requires an understanding of how all players will move, interact, and execute their responsibilities. Being the quarterback requires an awareness of what the other team plans to do in order to disrupt your play. I loved playing and now love watching football because I understand both the big picture and the small details of each down throughout the game. Having been surrounded by football from the time I was born, it is the sport that holds the most strategic interest to me and holds a place in my heart because it connects me to family memories.

A Dependable Leader

Who do I have to thank for my understanding of the game of football – my dad. He coached football my entire childhood. I remember being little, six or seven years old, and going with him to his youth football practices. At that age, the seventh- and eighth-grade players seem so big. A perk of being the coach's sons meant that my brothers and I could start playing a couple of years early. In fifth grade, I joined my older brother on the seventh-grade team and played for the Jayhawks. To be honest, I remember being pretty scared playing against older boys. I was pretty small, but after getting tackled for the first time, my dad recalls that I ran off the field with a smile and told him it didn't hurt at all. From then on, I was hooked.

In their book *Stick Together*, Jon Gordon and Kate Leavell share a story of a basketball team exploring and experiencing the challenges and the triumphs of working together as a team. Like my father, the basketball coach in the story understands the importance of modeling dependability. Gordon and Leavell write, "Leaders who show their teams they love them and care about them have more committed players. A team that loves each other is able to challenge each other to work harder and sacrifice more" (Gordon, 2021). For me, my passion for football wasn't just about the sport itself, it was the team aspect that I loved. I had a group of guys who were my friends, that I could trust to do the work needed to be successful. I had coaches I trusted would show up and help lead us to be our very best. Simply by being on the team, I had people I could depend on and who depended on me. Of course, this was not by accident – it was an intentional aspect of the sport that my dad and the other coaches emphasized.

I have spent years coaching Adam and his two brothers from t-ball through Little League, from youth wrestling to youth football – though, football is my number one sport. I spent twenty-one years as a certified youth football coach and it wasn't easy. Trying to teach the skills of playing football to young boys from fifth to eighth grade is daunting. Where to begin? We decided, as a coaching staff, that each of us needed to commit to the program and to the kids. We had to demonstrate the commitment we wanted them to make. Once we committed to that, we would then show our players what it meant to be dependable. We didn't directly talk to them about dependability. Rather, we showed them by being there every day, to listen, teach, and support every member of our team. Once they trusted that we were committed coaches, they were more willing to commit to themselves, to their teammates, and then to the program. Accountability came into play as the playbooks were handed out and each player was expected to learn his assignments for each play. After each player completed his assignment, they then needed to rely on each other to each do their part, making the team strong and reliable. Our seasons were never defined by wins or losses, but by how each player grew and therefore how the team grew from August to November – and they always made me proud.

A Rigorous Rhythm

The conductor steps up in front of the ensemble and taps her baton on the music stand. Sixty-four musicians sit up tall with their instruments prepared for what comes next. All eyes are on the conductor as she raises her baton. With military precision, the musicians raise their instruments to the ready. There is a silence in the moment before the conductor cues the musicians – a breath in unison as the baton goes up, and as it drops on the downbeat, the music comes to life. The percussionists drive the beat that keeps the entire ensemble together. The trumpets blare to grab the attention of the audience before backing off to allow the flutes to enter and float above the bass of the French horns, baritones, and tuba. The clarinets, oboes, and bassoons battle against the saxophones – back and forth, exchanging the melody between each other. The music grows and grows as each instrument is layered on top of one another, sending a wall of sound out into the audience that pushes them back in their seats. Fortissimo, as the conductor holds out her hands, slowly moving them out and up as the most beautiful note is powerfully sustained. A sharp swipe of the baton, and in an instant, silence. The musicians hold their positions as the final note lingers throughout the space. A perfectly executed piece of music.

In fifth grade, I began football and I also began band. Of course, there was only one instrument that I wanted to play. I was not content to play a bass line, so no trombone or baritone for me. I needed something with more bravado than a flute or clarinet. Yes, I knew right away that the trumpet was the instrument for me. Blaring and glimmering, it perfectly fit my young personality – and I played loud! If the written comments on the judge's assessment form for my fifth-grade Solo-Ensemble competition piece from 1991 are accurate, as a first-year musician, I needed to work on intonation, embouchure, and breathing – but I played with "a lot of energy and gusto." Yup, I've always had a loud enthusiasm in life. In my trumpet playing that enthusiasm came blaring through.

A Beautiful Bond

Of course, as I played in band with the rest of the musicians, I had to learn to control this gusto. On many occasions, my band director had to remind me that the dynamic markings were not suggestions. I needed to circle them in my music and follow them – in other words, everything was not played at fortissimo. This was an important lesson to learn. Our band was an ensemble – the artistic name for a "team" – and we were all connected to each other. In their book, Gordon and Leavell write, "When a team is connected they feel more committed to each other. We make connections by sharing who we are...and listening to each other" (Gordon, 2021). In grade-school band, each musician played an important role in the creation and performance of a piece of music. We needed to listen to each other and hear how our part connected to the whole piece. Yes, there were times that the trumpets got to shine as we played loudly in a specific section of the piece. Yet we needed to be mindful of the other musicians and when and how they got to shine, as well – playing softly to support their melody line. Most of the time, it was not about any solo musician or section commanding the spotlight, but rather the ensemble as a whole playing together in a way that seemed like one body of sound – balanced and beautiful. As my friend Amanda Gray, who is an incredible middle school band teacher, writes, when the band plays a piece of music, it is more than just one musician or even the ensemble as a whole. The music created includes the emotions, the growth, the confidence, and the trust that unify the ensemble that makes the piece truly a unique work of art.

I have always told my students that a band is like a team, except our word for team is ensemble. From the beginning of the school year, my band members learn what the term "ensemble" is and what it means to be a part of one. While introducing Purpose-Driven Learning in my middle school classroom, I found that teaching the Key of Dependability was easy for my students to relate to and understand. We often talk about how we are each an individual contributing to one ensemble working toward a common goal: making music together.

When you break it down, ensemble music is simply a variety of individual parts, written and designed to be performed together to create a musical experience. A recipe for a song, if you will. The performers themselves are what give life to the music. I explain to my students that when we are performing a piece, WE depend on THEM to know their part just like THEY depend on US to know ours. Through many hours of rehearsal, the performers learn and refine their individual parts to be played together with the entire ensemble – this is where the fun begins! Just like a puzzle, each part contributes to the beauty that is the final picture. It is during this journey of exploring the music where we learn so much about each other. Performers discover one another's strengths and rely on each other for support when faced with a challenge. Through time and practice, a level of trust is built within the ensemble that gives us the confidence to perform beyond what is written on the page. The final performance of a piece of music is more than just "playing a song." The final performance portrays the array of emotions from the challenges and successes of learning it, the camaraderie built from working together towards a common goal, and the pride of reaching the end of the journey for this particular piece.

Dependability is a Key of Purpose-Driven Learning that resonates in my classroom. My students learn the importance of being dependable through their unique roles and their purpose in our ensemble. In my opinion, one of the best parts about being in band is learning the value of being a part of a team and recognizing that, without you, the ensemble is not complete.

Two Sides of the Same Coin

Having been involved with both the arts and athletics from an early age, it always surprises me that people see these experiences as two different worlds. People are often surprised to know that I was both an athlete and an artist in middle and high school, as if a person can only be one or the other. At times, parents and schools unintentionally support this false dichotomy – labeling kids from an early age as sporty or artsy, athletic or creative. Certainly, as educators, we know that our students can be both. In fact, I think that it is important to encourage and empower our students to explore both. In many ways, they develop similar skills. Yet, in very distinct ways, they offer our students unique challenges and growth – one coin, two sides.

Both team sports and ensemble-based arts are amazing for building key social-emotional learning skills connected to collaboration and competition. Showing up, being prepared, working hard, communicating challenges, supporting struggles, and celebrating success are important aspects of teams and ensembles. Yet they are not exactly the same, and it is in the differences that I found unique enjoyment in both. You see, football, wrestling, and baseball have weekly competitions. My team and I prepared each week for the next challenge. Some weeks we won. Other weeks, we lost. Like my father said earlier in the chapter, it's not about the wins and losses, but anyone who has competed in sports knows that Monday's practice after a loss is different than after a win. Each new week brings another opportunity to reflect on the past week, make a plan for the coming week, practice the plan, and execute the plan come game time. In the arts, often the ensemble works for weeks, even months, for a single night or weekend. There is a slower build and a need for enduring dependability. Even at the start of the rehearsal process, each ensemble member must show up, put in the work, build on the skills learned before, and continue to develop, so that when the time comes the whole ensemble is ready. All of the planning and rehearsing culminate in a singular performance.

I am not here to say one is better than the other – in fact, I think both offer an interesting perspective on what is required to be a dependable teammate or ensemble member. In sports, athletes have a chance to reflect, make changes, and try again. There are weekly opportunities to demonstrate one's dependability and it can be built little by little throughout the season. In the arts, the performance very much feels like a "this is it" type of moment. There isn't the chance to do it over or try again next week. Certainly, dependability has been built little by little throughout the rehearsal process, but that "teamwork" is tested in one, big, "are you ready" moment. Both demonstrations of dependability are filled with trust, excitement, and connection – and I love them both!

Reflecting on Your Story

- ♦ Did you compete in sports or perform in the arts when in middle or high school? Do you consider yourself an athlete? How about an artist?
- ♦ How do you see being on a team or in an ensemble as similar? How are they different?
- ♦ Like in sports, how can your students demonstrate weekly dependability? Do they have opportunities to

The Key of Dependability ◆ 125

reflect, make changes, and try to grow in their dependability from class to class?

◆ Like in the arts, how can your students collaborate for a singular moment of dependability? How will you know, how will they know that, when it counts, they can be confident in being dependable?

Exploring Our "WHY"

Moonshot Dependability

Have you heard of moonshot thinking? It is the mindset that looks at the impossible and, instead of saying it can't be done, chooses to take on the challenge of making it possible. You know, like the vision people once shared of going to the moon. Yet, for all of the inspiration we can get from learning about moonshot thinkers and engaging in moonshot thinking, it takes actions to make the impossible possible. As we look throughout history at every great accomplishment, the needed actions were not undertaken by a single individual. The impossible was confronted by teams of like-minded individuals, who worked together to bring about the extraordinary. If moonshot thinking inspires imagination of what can be done, then it is moonshot dependability that takes action, unites a team, and keeps everyone committed until success is achieved.

In 1961, the United States was in a race with the Soviet Union to put a man on the moon. As the story is told, President John F. Kennedy was touring NASA headquarters late one evening and came across a janitor mopping the floor. JFK asked the janitor why he was working so late. The janitor replied, "Mr. President, I am helping put a man on the moon" (King, 2019). I love this story, and whether or not it is true, it is well documented that during this time most people, working all kinds of jobs at NASA, reported feeling a deep connection to the work of putting a man on the moon. It wasn't just the engineers or the astronauts. Everyone in the organization needed to be dependable and do their part in the work that was required to meet this shared goal. The work of the cleaning crew or the office staff or the cafeteria workers played a role in the success of the whole organization.

Does the waterboy know his importance to the overall success of the basketball team? How does the last chair violinist feel about her role in the overall success of the orchestra? In our classrooms, do our students feel that their individual dependability leads to the whole class achieving a level of greatness that some might consider impossible? Without a moonshot mission within our classroom, success remains individual – and the simple truth is that individual success is never as meaningful or impactful as the success of the whole team, ensemble, class, or community. Developing and demonstrating dependability becomes essential to our students moving beyond a desire for individualist gain and embracing a sense of communal connection and commitment. It is only through this connection and commitment that all of our students will be able to reach the moon.

All for One

In his book *You Are The Team*, Michael Rogers explores how to be a dependable team member from a different perspective than most "teamwork" books. Instead of speaking to the leaders of teams and offering insight on how leadership can develop a strong team, Rogers challenges each team member, writing that "great teams are made up of great teammates" (Rogers, 2017). How many of our students want to blame struggles and failures on others? It's their lab partner's fault that the project failed. It's the officials' fault that the team lost. It's the choreographer's fault because the dance was too hard. It is the teacher's fault and that's why they are not doing well in class. If our students can see our class as a kind of team, then Rogers' advice can be for them – what is their role in making the team "better" and how can they take responsibility in helping the team achieve greatness? Great classes are made up of great students.

Through Another's Eyes

We are constantly telling our students not to worry about what others think of them. It is how they view themselves that matters. Yet, if we are being honest – how others view them is important, especially when those people are part of their team or ensemble. Of course, I am not talking about how they are viewed by the mean girl who is jealous of their talent or the insecure jock who needs to bully others to feel big. Their meanness is not a perspective with which our students should concern themselves. However, the perspectives of the adults in leadership, their coaches, directors, and support staff certainly are valid. Their reputation within the communities they are a part of matters. When members of the team and ensemble voice constructive feedback, our students should listen and reflect. Does your coach see you as a dedicated and reliable player? Do the other people in the musical cast see you as hard-working, humble, and committed to the production? Does your boss at the grocery store respect your punctuality and work ethic? Do the people in your church appreciate your selfless service and positive attitude? Do loved ones at home trust that your words and actions will reflect positively on your family's reputation? In our classrooms, we can help develop the habits of our students that create their character – and it is their character that will demonstrate their dependability.

Inspiring Our Students' Stories

- How do your students demonstrate dependability beyond your classroom – sports, arts, clubs, work, home? How can you tap into that sense of dependability within your class?
- Do your students know the moonshot mission of your classroom?
- Do your students see themselves as essential members of the team needed to accomplish this mission?
- Avoiding guilt and shame, how can you hold your students accountable for their role in the whole class achieving their greatest success?

Unlocking and Empowering Purpose-Driven Dependability

"B" Dependable

Teams, ensembles, clubs, and classes in school that struggle often have similar challenges – a lack of commitment from those involved, selfishness in seeking personal success, egos that are often inflated by parental praise, little trust between participants, a lack of constructive peer feedback, gossip about others within the team, a lack of care and respect among the group, and, quite simply, no authentic interest in becoming better. Combating these obstacles is no easy task for a teacher, an advisor, a coach, or a director. Of course, the first step is to always model the character traits you wish to nurture in your students – like honesty, responsibility, care, and empathy. While not specifically speaking to educators, the 6 B's that Michael Rogers writes about in his book are six strategies for teachers and students that are beneficial in building dependability in any classroom, in any club, on any team, or within any ensemble. He challenges each individual student to take the initiative of creating a great classroom, saying, "Don't wait for your leader or other teammates to make it happen. YOU make it happen" (Rogers, 2017).

How do we achieve greatness within our classroom? The answer lies in inspiring and motivating our students to make the commitment to become great members of the class.

Be Selfless and Be Trustworthy

In the United States, we live in a highly individualistic society. Our students enter our classrooms with a cultural perspective that encourages individual success at all costs. Schools do not help overcome this ideology; rather, they support it with graded systems that seek to pit our students against one another for academic status – honor roll, National Honors Society, and class ranking all based on getting higher grades than other students. Right from the start, educators are challenged when seeking to intentionally develop dependability within their classroom. For dependability to thrive one must take a step back from individual pursuits in order to reflect on the needs of the group. The goal of our classroom cannot be "to get an A." It must be rooted in collaboration and a shared vision of greatness. Our students must be willing to demonstrate their trustworthiness by contributing to the success of the class and must be willing to trust that others will also work toward the good of all.

In this type of classroom, the highest-achieving students take the initiative to help other students who are struggling. Students volunteer to take on additional tasks that need to be completed. Students see other students making the commitment to success and are motivated to demonstrate the same level of commitment. There is follow-through in actions, communication when challenges are faced, and an openness to feedback for continued growth.

Be Positive and Be Respectful

As when we explored the Key of Enthusiasm, I love that Rogers writes about the power of positivity. A positive mindset goes a long way in creating a successful team. It is crucial for the teacher to model this mindset. There will be challenges, members of the team will disagree, and every now and then the class may take a step back. However, in these times, all members of the team must remain respectful to one another and strive to maintain a positive perspective on the future.

In my home, as we gather around the dining room table for dinner, we often share our highs and lows – though we call them the roses and thorns. We even have taken to naming a rosebud – something we are looking forward to tomorrow, a possible future rose. Have your students respectfully share their frustration with the work accomplished in that class period. Have them find a positive at the end of each class – even if that positive is simply that the team got through their time together. Tomorrow is a new day, which may need to begin with apologies, accountability, and a plan to move forward. But if the team is still together, the mission can still be accomplished.

Be Humble and Be Great

A mission of greatness may sound arrogant – I mean, who am I to begin on a journey of greatness? However, understanding this mission requires the opposite of arrogance – humility is needed.

No one in our class, on our team, in our ensemble can achieve the level of greatness we are set out to accomplish on their own. We must work together as one in order to achieve impossible greatness. Start with humility and then set a clear goal.

In Drama, establishing a shared goal was not difficult. Putting on an amazing performance was our common mission, and I could remind students of this goal whenever teenage drama created conflict. For a sports team, it is often winning, making the playoff, and maybe even the championship. Even students with vast differences will come together and depend on one another in the pursuit of greatness. Now, a great performance or winning the championship is like the goal of putting a man on the moon – it is a big goal that is only achieved by a series of smaller, perhaps even more meaningful goals. In the pursuit of greatness, we nurture teamwork, awareness, empathy, respect, and resilience.

So – we must encourage our students to actively participate. In order to actively and constructively contribute, they must do the work needed to prepare. When a student doesn't prepare and therefore cannot contribute, it is not simply their success that will suffer. The entire class is less because they could not be trusted to prepare for class. When a student chooses to be disruptive, their behavior is not only detracting from their growth. It is detracting from the growth of the entire class. It may be a fine line, but we are not trying to guilt or shame our students into being dependable. Rather, we are seeking to raise their awareness of how their actions affect the whole. We want them to understand that they have a unique contribution to offer and their contribution is needed and expected. We want them to respect the work others are putting in and match it with their own effort. And we need them to know that mistakes and missteps can be overcome by the team as we continue to pursue our mission. We can use Rogers' words when speaking to our students: "Only you can personally commit to using your uniqueness and talents to help drive your team to greatness" (Rogers, 2017). A sold-out crowd and a standing ovation, or hoisting up the championship trophy, winning the state meet, or being recognized as the best school in the district – the moonshot mission must require the commitment of each person in the class, team, club, or ensemble. In the pursuit of perhaps superficial greatness, we are helping our students discover, nurture, and contribute their innate greatness to the world.

References

Gordon, J. and Leavell, K. (2021). *Stick Together: A Simple Lesson to Build a Stronger Team.* 1st ed. Hoboken: Wiley.

King, J. (2019). *How Great Leaders Communicate Big Vision So That Others Want to Join In.* Retrieved 21 November 2021, from https://medium.com/@Jude.M/how-great-leaders-communicate-big-vision-so-that-others-want-to-join-in-d3296e7ca37e.

Rogers, M. (2017). *You Are the Team: 6 Simple Ways Teammates Can Go from Good to Great.* Cedar City: CreateSpace Independent Publishing Platform.

9

The Key of Curiosity: Exploring the Wonder Within Each Day

Connecting to My Story

Who's This Guy?

"Good morning, everyone – please take your seats, stop talking, and give me your attention. I am Mr. Moreno and I'll be covering your class today." I turned down the music that was playing on my Bluetooth speaker when they came in. It's always something upbeat and inspirational, usually "Walking On Sunshine" by Katrina and the Waves or "I Feel Good" by James Brown.

"Your teacher has left instructions on what we are doing today, so let's take attendance and then we can get started. Beginning here in the front row, please take a breath, stand, make eye contact with me, and share your name and a greeting of your choice. I, in turn, will greet you using your name." Chatter breaks out, I see eyes roll, a few looks of panic, and then one brave soul challenges me – "Why?" or "Do we have to?"

"I would like you to. I've been doing this a long time and I have found there is great value in connecting with each of you, by name, even if I am only here for today. I want you to know that I see you. I want you to feel like a part of this class today. And I want us to take a step forward in confidently speaking, at least our name, into the world. I would like everyone to share with me their name, but I'll take volunteers to start."

The students look around – who is going to be first? Having taken a seat on the stool at the front of the classroom, I offer to demonstrate first. I take a deep breath and stand. "Good morning, everyone. I am Mr. Moreno." Silence. "Ah, friends, when someone offers you a greeting, it is kind to offer one back. Good morning, everyone." And while not everyone responds, I am amazed at the number of students who do – "Good morning, Mr. Moreno." A few students volunteer to go before we begin to go up and down the rows.

"Good morning, Mr. Moreno. My name's Michael."

"Good morning, Michael – Michael is the name of my best friend. Good name."

"I'm Anna. Good morning, Mr. Moreno."

"Good morning, Anna. Teachers are not supposed to admit to having favorites, but Anna is the name of one of my favorite students of all time."

"Hey, I'm Will."

"Good morning, Will – I am going to ask that you do that once more standing and making eye contact, please."

"Oh yeah, sorry, I forgot."

"No problem – just try again."

"Hey, I'm Will. How are you doing today?"

"Hey, Will – I am doing great! Thank you for being willing to do it again. Glad you are here this morning."

Only two students out of twenty-eight refuse to stand and it is clear that this type of exercise is beyond where they are currently at. For attendance sake, I ask them to still share with me their names from their seats and I offer them a quick greeting. The spotlight is not where these two will shine today and that's OK.

"Alright, everyone – can someone please share with me what class this is and what you are learning." And with that, we begin a non-traditional time of learning together.

Who Ya Gonna Call?

Since returning to the educational world, I have had the opportunity to speak about the power of Purpose-Driven Learning

(PDL) at conferences all over the country. I have led professional development workshops, working with other educators from a variety of content areas who work with all different age groups. PDL has a way of connecting with people and offering opportunities to discuss the challenges of our traditional educational systems and explore possible strategies for transforming the process of teaching and learning. Yet, for me to be relevant, for me to be able to speak from authentic experience, I must continue to seek out opportunities to be in classrooms working directly with students – and so, I am a substitute teacher!

The demand for substitute teachers never seems to dwindle – in fact, if I was able to, I could sub every day of the school year at the handful of schools within my community. This demand is a blessing for me, but a real challenge for schools. For me, there are so many options available – most weeks, I have my choice of grade level and subject area. At this point in the book, it should surprise no one that I like to mix it up and try new areas and new ages. The challenge for schools is the number of under-qualified substitute teachers out there. In my home state of Wisconsin, there is such a need for teachers that becoming a substitute only requires a college degree (in anything) and a three-day course. I am thankful for folks who are willing to take on the difficult work of substitute teaching, but it becomes a lot harder when you don't have formal teaching education and experience. It also is a challenge in the classroom for the students who look to the teacher for learning and for structure. That said, I am thankful to be a trained, experienced teacher as I enter classrooms as a substitute.

Now teachers, you do not always support the work of the substitute teacher covering in your absence. In my years of substitute teaching, I have had the full range of teacher preparedness. I have had complete, detailed lesson plans, some even with time lengths for each part of the lesson. On the other end, I have gone into classrooms with no lesson plan and not even knowing what subject I was covering. I was once told by an assistant principal, as he walked me from the class I was supposed to cover to a new classroom, "Just get them through the period without having to call down to the office." That was fun.

I am so thankful to have the diverse experiences I have. They truly have prepared me to enter any classroom and engage students in meaningful ways. As we look back at the story which began this chapter, I hope you see a number of valuable strategies I use as a sub. First and foremost, I want to quickly establish that this day, the day I am subbing in this classroom, will be different than when the other teacher is here. By establishing that today will be different, I seek to spark the students' curiosity from the moment they enter. I want the students' normal routine to be disrupted. I want them asking – "Who is this guy?"

Music is a fun way to accomplish this. Even though I talk about the power of music all the time, very few teachers actually implement this strategy. When students of any age walk into a classroom in which my music is playing, they are curious – "What is going on?"

Once they are wondering, curious about the differences, for at least this moment, I have their full attention. And with that, I engage them with the strategies of PDL. What better place to put into practice the very techniques I teach educators in my workshops than in the classrooms in which I substitute teach. I can focus the class by having them take mindful breaths. In a small way, I can build students' confidence by having them stand and share their names. I can connect through intentional eye contact. I can begin to create a space of belonging by affirming each student and letting them know that I see them and that their presence and voice are needed contributions in this space. Does it take up fifteen minutes of class that was not in the lesson plan – yup. But no content is more important than establishing a connection, taking a step forward in building relationship, and even if just for this moment, nurturing each student's sense of value and worth.

I wish this was how most classes would begin. I wish that entering to music, a supportive space of inclusion in which students can confidently share their voice, was not strange to them. I wish it was the norm – but sadly, it is not. So when a substitute comes to cover the class and engages the students in this manner, they are curious.

Now this might sound a little self-serving and, perhaps, I need to explore more "educationally sound" language around what I am about to say – but the truth is, school communities hold little expectations around what a sub does with students or is able to accomplish with them. "Here is a lesson – do what you can." "There is no lesson – do what you can." I decided pretty quickly in my substitute teaching career that I will take a different approach than most substitute teachers take in the classrooms I am in. Yes, I will try my best to cover the content of a lesson plan if one is provided. But I will present content with non-traditional tools and I will engage students with the strategies of PDL.

As a former Drama teacher, it is not challenging for me to engage rather quickly with most students. I am pretty out-going, I have a lot of energy, and I like to think that I am rather funny. Coming from teaching in a non-traditional classroom, my behavior management skills are relatively strong, and after years of using PDL, many of the strategies are simply how I teach and engage others.

In my years of using this pedagogy, one thing holds true – a Purpose-Driven approach sparks curiosity. Once the students' curiosity is sparked, I need to fan the flames and continue to inspire their interest and participation. This looks a little different depending on the classroom, the content, and the age group. However, no matter the context, wonder can be motivating and curiosity can certainly drive engagement and learning.

Curiosity of the Young

I love working with students of every age. Of course, each grade level has its challenges. Yet each also has its unique joys. When I substitute teach in elementary school, I love the instant welcome that I feel. It feels like every student is excited to see me and wants to be my helper for the day. I love the freedom and openness with which they express themselves. So often, they are not yet bound by a fear of looking "uncool." They share their enthusiasm for school proudly and they are eager to jump into learning. They ask a million questions and they seem so curious about the new lesson.

This was the reality of one such third-grade class that I had the opportunity to substitute teach in for two consecutive days. One of the lessons I was asked to prepare ahead of time was for math. These students were exploring measurements and I was to cover how to use a ruler and yardstick to take linear measurements. The teacher had a nice handout with measurement terms and definitions. The handout also had a list of things that the students were to measure with their ruler or yardstick and record. Now, the students may have had fun all measuring the same things with the same tools, but I had a slightly different approach.

On the first day, I shared with the students a number of "old-time" measuring terms. The pyramids were measured in cubits, which are measured from the tip of the middle finger to the elbow. A knight's horse was measured in spans, which is the distance between one's pinky and thumb. A foot was measured simply by a person's foot and a yard was the length of an arrow. With this knowledge, I set the students free to measure anything and everything and record it in their journals. It was so fun seeing their curiosity flourish. How many cubits high was the door? How many feet was the classroom? Every student wanted to know how many spans tall they were. Once they were done, we came back together and they shared their findings. The students quickly realized that even though they had measured many of the same things, they all had various measurements recorded. Was the door five or six cubits high? Was the classroom eighteen or twenty feet long? And, by golly, six kids measured Aiden and got six different span heights. Without me teaching it, completely based on their own experience, these students agreed that we needed a standardized system for measurement. This agreement made for an actual cheer the next day when I brought out the rulers and yardsticks. Now as the students explored inches, feet, and yards, they sought precision and understood the value of the tools they were using. There is joy in discovery. Let's let our students follow their curiosity to discovery – even if they discover that which has already been discovered.

Collaboratively Curious

Perhaps one of my favorite experiences of substitute teaching occurred in an eighth-grade science lab. I had the opportunity to teach the class for the entire week, as the teacher was on an extended professional development trip. The science teacher had done a nice job outlining the lab she wanted me to lead and wanted her students to experience – making and testing "homemade" thermometers. Now, I have never made my own thermometer, so before the students arrived for my first class, I followed the directions and successfully created one. If I am being honest, I was super excited when I moved the test tube from the cold water into the hot water and watched the red-dyed rubbing alcohol rise up through the clear straw. It worked and I was pumped.

As the students came in, I played "Hot, Hot, Hot" by Buster Poindexter, introduced myself and the cool lab project, then had the students introduce themselves. The first day, I gave the students all of the needed supplies to assemble their thermometers, but did not give them any directions on how to build them. The teacher had said that they had already learned the concepts needed to understand the lab and the students confirmed this knowledge in our discussion. On the first day, I wanted to see which students could apply their understanding to the mechanical assembly of a thermometer. It was fun to watch – each lab pairing tested and re-tested various prototypes. As students grew frustrated and wanted me to simply tell them how, I played dumb. After all, I was "just the sub." Since I acted like I didn't know the answer, I was able to model curiosity. I asked "wondering" questions. "I wonder how we can get the pressure inside the test tube to push the rubbing alcohol up the straw?" At the end of the first class, very few students successfully made a thermometer. "Don't worry, folks – I'll be back again tomorrow and will give it another try."

At the beginning of the second class, I was amazed at how many students "magically" knew how to build a thermometer. Most students confessed to looking up the answer the night before and apologized. But I told them not to be sorry – they were curious and they sought out the answer. That is what schools should be encouraging. In every class, the students who learned the proper way assisted the students who still didn't know. They "taught" me and as I pretended not to understand, they explained and re-explained both the how and the why – how to build it and why it works. On the third and fourth days, they finished their lab reports, complete with a hand-drawn picture of their thermometer that labeled and explained each step in the process. Several of the students took the initiative to finish a gamified "sidequest," as well – borrowing a few supplies to run and record the experiment at home with their families. Exploring their curiosity in class and then helping to spark curiosity at home – pretty amazing.

Combatting Educational Apathy

My struggle with high school students is that so many of them have become apathetic to their own learning. "I don't know" or "I don't care" seem to be many of their mantras. Now, I strongly believe that this is the fault of schools, so I don't blame students for their indifference. Yet my goal is to challenge this attitude and, in my time with them, chip away at it in order to remind them of the joy of caring and engaging. In my fight against indifference and apathy, sparking curiosity is my number one strategy. Wondering requires caring. Questioning requires engagement.

I used these tools in a sophomore English class in which I substituted. They were finishing Macbeth, content that was right in my wheelhouse. The lesson plan was simple – have the students explain to me the plot, characters, and themes. Basically, a teach-the-substitute lesson to help them prepare for the test. Like with the middle school class, I could have played dumb and had them share with me the details, but I rarely do what I am told. Instead of "playing dumb" and spending a class period trying to pull answers from students or having the same three students answer all of my questions, I tried a different strategy. As the students entered to the soundtrack from *Game of Thrones*, the directions on the board asked them to sit quietly and write the Shakespearean quote that was on the board in their notebooks: "Tomorrow, and tomorrow, and tomorrow, creeps in this petty pace from day to day, to the last syllable of recorded time" (Shakespeare, 1606/2013, 5.5).

Once the bell rang, I began, without introduction or preface, Macbeth's monologue after the death of his wife in Act 5. Whether it was true interest or absolute surprise or maybe simple confusion – the whole class was silent for the entire recitation. At the end, they actually applauded me and one student asked, "Who are you?" I shared with them who I was and some of my theatrical distinctions, including the years I spent teaching young actors the very play they had just finished reading. You see, I did not engage their curiosity by playing dumb. I sparked it by demonstrating my expertise.

In true teenage fashion, several wanted to question this expertise – did this sub really know everything about Macbeth? Do I know everything about Macbeth – certainly not, but I knew more than a bunch of sixteen-year-olds. I humored a few questions to establish my knowledge, then broke them into groups. I handed each group three index cards that had an act, a scene, and a question. They had thirty minutes to review the scene, discuss it, and answer the questions, backing up their answer with material from the play. In the second half of the class, we shared answers. "Who was responsible for Macbeth's death?" Group one answered MacDuff, having reviewed Act 5 Scene 8. Group two answered the witches after reviewing Act 1 Scene 1. Group three, having reviewed Act 5, Scene 5, decided Macbeth is responsible. Group four wanted to blame Lady Macbeth after reviewing Act 1, Scene 7, and Group five agreed, having reviewed Act 2, Scene 2.

The debate that arose was awesome! Their curiosity had been set ablaze as the groups came to different conclusions for every question. As one group would answer differently, almost all of the students would quickly turn to that act and scene to look it over and try to refute the answer given. "No one is responsible for Macbeth's actions, except for Macbeth." "Macbeth wanted to stop, but Lady Macbeth made him continue." "It can't be Lady Macbeth, she is already dead when Macbeth dies." "Macduff is the one who killed him." "Macduff may have killed Macbeth, but the witches' predictions led him to that point." "The witches didn't predict his death. They just know that when men thirst for power, people die." Ooo – good point.

Several times in our discussion, they would look to me for the "right" answer. I shared with them that there wasn't a "right or wrong" answer to the questions I posed. That their answers were valid if they could defend them with evidence from the script. I, of course, did share a few suggestions for how we can understand this Shakespearean play and ended the class sincerely praising them for their effort and engagement. Their teacher wanted me to review the who and the what of the play. I sought to engage their curiosity by allowing them the opportunity to wonder and explore the why and the how – wondering why these characters and events are important to the overall themes of the play, wondering how the characters' words and actions influenced the plot and moved the story forward.

Reflecting on Your Story

- ◆ What sparks your curiosity? What are the things you "wonder" about?
- ◆ When you cannot explain something or don't know the answer to a question, how do you go about finding answers?
- ◆ Do you see yourself as the "expert" in your classroom? How does this perspective of your expertise influence your teaching?
- ◆ Who in your learning or in your life models curiosity? How in their words or actions do they express their curiosity?

Exploring Our "WHY"

Curiosity Takes Flight

Over the many years of using the Keys of PDL in my work with young people, I have come to more fully understand the value of each. However, if I'm being honest, that was not always the case.

In the early years, while curiosity made the list, I never really thought much of it. In my conversations with students, I would emphasize the significance of being a creative individual, the need to be a confident leader, and, especially in my middle school Drama classroom, the importance of being a focused and dependable ensemble member. Curiosity was on the list so that I didn't have to answer students' questions – "Hmmm, great question, Bobby. You know, curious learners take the initiative to discover the answers for themselves." Worked every time. But in all seriousness, curiosity was not one of the keys that I valued as much as the others. That is until I heard Elizabeth Gilbert, author of *Eat, Pray, Love* and *Big Magic*, speak about a Curiosity-Driven Life (similarity of name is a surprising coincidence). She said, "If you can let go of passion and follow your curiosity, your curiosity might lead you to your passion" (Gilbert, 2015, 26.14).

Like her, I am a "passion-driven" individual. As such, certain Keys of PDL held more weight. One must pursue their passion with confidence – there is little room for doubt when one is fully committed. Success in one's passion is achieved when an enthusiastic attitude meets a resilient determination. As with Gilbert, I declared the importance of a passion-driven, "jack-hammer" pursuit of greatness. Curiosity, I thought, was for those who hadn't found their passion, yet…not for me. And, like her, as I reflected on my teaching, I realized that I needed to transform this perspective.

In listening to Gilbert's presentation, two things dawned on me. First, it's not about me. It's about my students. While some of my students may have discovered their passion at an early age, most had not. Curiosity should not be at the bottom of my list. It needed to be at the top. Like the hummingbird Gilbert describes in her presentation, I want students to fly from interest to interest, getting a taste of a little bit of everything – discovering new things, creatively "cross-pollinating" between interests, and developing a beautiful diversity of skills. I don't want them deciding in middle school what their passion is. I want their passion to be exploration. I want their passion to be risk-taking. I want their passion to be learning as much as they can about as many things as they can. I want their passion to be curiosity!

My second realization was that the choice between jack-hammer passion and hummingbird curiosity is not an "either–or" decision. It is, as we will explore with the Key of Resilience, a "both–and" opportunity. Like a hummingbird, we encourage our students to continually explore and discover. Yet, we must encourage jack-hammer focus and effort as they seek to develop skills and grow in their abilities. It is actually how I believe that I have found joy and meaning in my life, so far: pursuing my passion for sports in middle and high school, discovering a passion for the arts and pursuing them in college, exploring my passion for the outdoors at camp, and a decade later "flying over" to ministry to "cross-pollinate" my skills as an innovative teacher with my vocation as a pastor. Curiosity has driven me to explore a diverse number of interests. Once discovered, I have pursued them with a fervent passion as I have worked for excellence in each. I guess it is what I now want for our students – to help them become hummingbirds with jack-hammers.

A Compass to Guide the Way

Elizabeth Gilbert encourages us to be driven by our curiosity in the pursuit of discovering our passion. Whether passion-driven, curiosity-driven, or even Purpose-Driven – being driven can be exhausting and, if not careful, can become an all-consuming ambition. In the pursuit of our passion, we must be mindful of our mental health and well-being. In the discovery, development, and demonstration of their innate greatness, our students must be mindful of their holistic wellness. Curiosity is an important aspect of this mindfulness. Scott Stoner and Holly Hughes Stoner of the Samaritan Family Wellness Foundation might say that being curiosity-driven allows a person the space and time to explore their mental health and whole-person wellness in a more intentional manner.

These two incredible people are both licensed marriage and family therapists and are the founders of The Wellness Compass Initiative. Their resources offer people the opportunity to self-assess one's wellness in eight essential areas on the Wellness Compass: healthy relationships, handling emotions, rest and play, spirituality, vocation, organization, resilience, and care for the body. Once assessed, trained facilitators offer Wellness Circles – a gathering with others who have taken the self-assessment inventory. The participants are interested in journeying together in the "watering of their garden" and the intentional focus and growth within an area of wellness. The self-assessment inventory and the Wellness Circles are designed specifically for different groups and are offered for adults, parents, teens, and kids. Here's what Holly has to say about their work using the compass with teens, families, and in schools.

It seems that people of all ages tend to go through life in a somewhat haphazard way, often believing that life happens to them and that the best they can do is ride the waves. We try to help adults, parents, and students see that when they stop and are curious about their daily choices and curious about how things could be, they can proactively make changes that more fully support their mental health and their overall well-being.

When we work within school communities, we find that students, parents, and staff alike enjoy the chance to stop and be more thoughtful about their well-being. Taking one of our assessments (adult, parent, teen/kid) brings them a greater awareness of their daily habits in eight different areas of wellness, and it helps them feel more hopeful. They imagine how their life might be different and more under their control, if they were more intentional in "watering certain areas of their wellness garden," as we say. They also are curious about how the changes they want for themselves could affect other positive changes in their lives, and they begin to feel empowered.

With shared vocabulary around mental health and well-being, different populations within an institution can speak more efficiently about what is healthy and what is challenging to health within their setting. Again, members of the community might be curious about what changes they could make to support increased health and well-being for all involved. As you can see, curiosity drives the entire process.

I have had the honor of being trained as a Wellness Circle facilitator and have been a participant in several circles myself. Like a substitute teacher, the facilitator doesn't have all the answers and must ask questions to help the circle explore, reflect, and discover on their own with the support of the group. We journey together only for a short time. Yet the impact can be great when being driven by curiosity leads to mindfulness, wonder, awareness, and action. If we are going to take Elizabeth Gilbert's advice and encourage our students to let their curiosity drive them, then having a compass to guide their journey is a perfect fit.

Inspiring Our Students' Stories

- ♦ How do your students express their curiosity within your classroom?
- ♦ What are specific strategies you use for inspiring your students' wonder and curiosity?
- ♦ What passions do your students have beyond your classroom that you can encourage them to bring into your classroom and connect to your content?
- ♦ How can you encourage and praise questions, exploration, and wondering within your teaching and your students' learning?

Unlocking and Empowering Purpose-Driven Curiosity

Playing Dumb

Even when I was a full-time Drama teacher, this was one of my favorite go-to strategies for encouraging students to become more curious. They are so used to teachers answering questions for them – I didn't. Sometimes, I would simply tell them that they needed to put forth the effort of finding the answers to their questions. But it was always fun to pretend like I had no clue. As a Drama teacher, I like to think that my acting was impeccable. I always loved when students then discovered the answers on their own and came back to me to "teach" me so I knew.

Of course, this strategy needs to be used sparingly. Sure, it works for me as I go into classrooms as a substitute teacher because no one is expecting me to be an expert in any specific content area.

In younger grades, it takes a little more pretending, acting like you are struggling so that your students can use their knowledge to help teach you. In the older grades, perhaps your students may actually ask questions to which you don't know the answer. Model curiosity when faced with a lack of knowledge. It is OK not to know – take the initiative to explore and find the answer. Model wonder and the enthusiasm of discovering something new.

Wonder With

The language of learning we use in our classrooms matters. I encourage you to move away from "right and wrong" language. You can nurture curiosity and higher-level thinking by modeling curiosity and asking students how they got a certain answer or why they believe their answer is correct. Instead of telling a student that their response is "wrong," I love using the word "wonder." "I wonder what would happen if we tried a different method" or "I wonder how you came to that conclusion." There is no shame in trying to learn and failing to know. Instead of being wrong, perhaps when students fail to arrive at the intended destination, we can wonder with them where in their thinking they took a misstep, headed in a different direction, or veered off on a creative detour.

Less Is More

Give fewer directions. Give fewer instructions. Give fewer answers. Give fewer restrictions. When I started to offer my students less, they took the initiative and began to do more. I'll admit that it is a tricky balance. Certainly, we need to offer our students enough to understand and move forward. However, too often, we restrict curiosity and creativity by giving them so much, there is little to no room for exploration. They simply need to take the prepared path – stay on the path that the teacher has prepared and arrive at the "A." Unfortunately, when our more "free-thinking" and creative students flitter away, following their curiosity to the many fascinating flowers beyond the prepared path, they are reprimanded and arrive at a failing destination. In turn, more limitations and more instructions are forced upon these hummingbird spirits until they no longer are able to fly. So sad, and yet too often the reality of our school structure.

Offer freedom and encourage exploration by stepping back and trusting that our students' curiosity will drive them to discover, create, and share.

Cliffhangers

Think of the final episode of a season for any hit show – the episode wraps up several of the plot points that had been explored all season. Yet, right at the end, they hit you with a shocker, something that makes you excited for the next season. As a huge Marvel superhero movie fan, it is the post-credit scenes that pique my interest and make me eager for the next movie. Actually, more than passive eagerness, my curiosity drives me to look up information about the scene. What does it mean? What does it reveal about upcoming movies? How does it connect to the comic books?

Suspense is another technique I often used in my classroom – sometimes planned, but often a result of my horrible time management skills. Stop at a point of excitement and engagement in order to encourage students to follow their curiosity beyond your classroom and return to the next class with discoveries. End a lesson early, so you can begin the next class at a peak moment of engaged learning – giving students just a taste of what is to come. Plan lessons as puzzle pieces that only reveal a small portion of a bigger picture – then make sure to offer a chance to assemble all the pieces to discover the masterpiece. Instead of wrapping each lesson up in a tidy little bow, I encourage teachers to keep the learning open, in order to keep students on the edge of their seats, eager to take additional steps forward.

References

Gilbert, E. (2015, October). *Elizabeth Gilbert: Flight of the Hummingbird: A Curiosity-Driven Life.* [Video]. Super Soul Session. www.elizabethgilbert.com/video/.

Samaritan Family Wellness Foundation. (2021). Retrieved 19 November 2021, from www.samaritanfamilywellness.org.

Shakespeare, W. (2013). *Macbeth.* B. Mowat & P. Werstine (Eds.). New York: Simon & Schuster. (Original work published 1606).

10

The Key of Empathy: Compassion, Curiosity, Connection

Connecting to My Story

A Universal Language

I am ordained as a pastor within the Evangelical Lutheran Church in America (ELCA). I identify as a Christian and my faith is at the center of who I am and how I engage with others. In this chapter, I am going to explore empathy through the lens of my faith and my work with children, teens, and young adults within the context of my ministry. However, I pray that my insight offers more than just my Christian perspective. I hope that it is a lens through which we can embrace our shared humanity – and in this book, I hope my perspective inspires others to explore empathy within our school communities. Indeed, empathy – compassion for others, respect for others, love for others – is not only a Christian value. It is a core tenet of all major religions. It is even at the core of secular society as we teach our children and strive to live by the Golden Rule: *"Do unto others as you would have them do unto you"* (Wattles, 1996).

DOI: 10.4324/9781003294634-11

In the Christian faith, we look to the teachings of Jesus Christ, who said: *"These things I command you, that you love one another"* (*New Revised Standard Version*, 1989/2009, John 15:17).

Ancient Taoism states: *"Regard your neighbor's gain as your gain, and your neighbor's loss as your loss"* (Taiqing, 2015).

In Judaism, the Torah offers a similar command from Yahweh: *"You shall love your neighbor as yourself, for I am the Lord"* (*The Torah*, 1962/1992, Leviticus 19:18b).

Buddhism speaks of the Golden Mean: *"Do not unto others what you would not they should do unto you. Then there will be no resentment against you, either in family or in the state"* (*The Analects of Confucius*, 1999, 12.2).

The prophet of Islam speaks this truth to his followers as recorded in the hadith: *"Seek for mankind that of which you are desirous for yourself, that you may be a believer"* (Shah, 2018).

And Hinduism shifts from simply a belief to one's duty: *"This is the sum of duty; do naught unto others what you would not have them do unto you"* (Krishnamacharya, 1983, 2012).

The belief, the command, the duty of all major religions, and even a core value of many people not connected to an organized religion, is rooted in an intentional love for others. As I continue with my story of ministry and the powerful empathy I have experienced from others and sought to nurture within myself, I hope that all who read this might find a connection. This is not a Christian story. I believe it is a universal story that speaks to the power of empathic love. Preaching this message has had an impact on my congregation members, especially the youth. Teens and young adults are seeking to connect with something greater than themselves. Empathy for themselves, for others, and for the world can connect them to our shared humanity and our sacred unity. How might our schools be transformed, if our whole community sought to live by a mission of showing empathic love to one another?

Pastor School

Seminary, as pastor school is officially called, is an institution of higher learning. In 2018, I got my master's degree in divinity from what is now called United Lutheran Seminary in

Philadelphia and Gettysburg, Pennsylvania. It was a lot of work – but the experience changed me, opened my eyes and my heart to the world in new ways, and gave me the knowledge and the empathy to engage others with more curiosity and compassion.

I am thankful to have grown up Lutheran, but did not really understand what it meant to be Lutheran until seminary. I knew the story: In his study of the holy scripture, a Catholic monk in Germany named Martin Luther began to question the teachings and practices of the church. Growing up, I thought that he decided to speak out against the false teachings and corrupt practices, left the Catholic Church, and started his own Christian denomination with his followers, the Lutherans. The reality offers much more depth to Luther's questioning of what he was taught to believe, his openness to understanding sacred scripture in a new way, his struggle to reconcile his new perspective with traditional practices, and his efforts to reform, not leave, the church. This changed my perception of Martin Luther and his mission, from that of confrontational revolt to empathic reform, which makes sense because every October 31st, the Lutheran Church celebrates The Reformation – the day we remember and honor Luther for his efforts to bring about needed change.

Reforming Our Judgment

In many of these chapters, I speak of my strengths in the social-emotional skill being explored. I am a confident and creative person, I have an enthusiastic attitude most of the time. I take the initiative to put forth my best effort, and when that effort fails, I rely on a resilient spirit to get me back on my feet and moving forward. As we explored focus, I shared my challenges and now as we explore empathy, I must once again confess my shortcomings. I am not the shoulder people come to cry on. My friends and family come to me for solutions, for tough feedback, and for honest advice. I fix problems and like to think that I help people become "better." This "fixer" mentality, at times, prevents me from actively listening and being empathically present. Often people are not looking for solutions, feedback, or advice. They are simply looking for a caring presence. I can also be confrontational with certain types of people. It is not that I am mean or don't care about them – certainly, I do. I just struggle with patience for those who are willfully ignorant, apathetic, or close-minded. I judge behavior that I perceive as laziness, indifference, or discriminatory. Instead of seeing our shared humanity and asking why their perspective or behaviors are frustrating me, I judge them as dumb, weak, or mean, struggle to respect them, and then choose to not engage with them.

OK, so that doesn't sound very pastoral – but then again, I haven't always been a pastor. The only way this book remains authentic is if I share with you my strengths and my limitations. It took leaving the comfort of my suburban life, teaching at a private prep school in the Midwest, my home where I was born and raised, to offer me a different approach to engaging others in more empathic ways. The ELCA is a progressive faith community, and in seminary I met people from many religions, various walks of life, and vastly different lived experiences than me. On the first day of my seminary orientation, I had the opportunity to meet many of the professors that I would have in the upcoming years. It was at this time that one of my professors gave me what I consider to be the best advice I have ever gotten. She told me that a meaningful seminary education is going to challenge my core beliefs and understanding of who God is, how God is revealed, and how I am called to be in relationship with God, with others, and with all of creation. She encouraged that when confronted with new learning and different perspectives, I needed to intentionally shift from my judgment to empathic curiosity. Judgment, she warned, shuts down an experience of God. Empathic curiosity opens us up to a transformative experience of the divine.

I was challenged during my time in seminary, but I believe that I was curious when confronted with contrary teaching and unfamiliar theologies. I had only ever been taught the perspective of old, European, male theologians. Exploring and learning to empathize with the theologies of female theologians, theologians of color, and LGBTQIA+ theologians was truly a challenging, yet sacred experience. In my Public Theology class, we visited differing faith communities and established inter-faith connections with Jewish people, Muslims, Hindus, and

Buddhists. Experiencing their services of worship and listening to their teachings moved my spirit and offered me new insight into my understanding of what connects us all to each other. What I gained in my seminary experience is a very Lutheran perspective – continual reformation. What I know today must grow and adapt as I explore new perspectives and ways of thinking. How I engage people today must develop and change as I empathize with the feelings and beliefs of others. Who I am today must continually reform as I encounter God in and through each new experience. Continual reformation requires curiosity and curiosity nurtures empathy.

Starting with Self-Empathy

After my first year in seminary, I headed off to Portland, Oregon to begin my twelve-week CPE internship. Clinical Pastoral Education is required pastoral care training as a chaplain within the context of a hospital or health care clinic. Along with completing rounds and being on call as a hospital chaplain, interns were required to participate in group discussions about their experiences, reflections on the work we were doing, and extensive self-reflection of our blind spots, growing edges, and triggers.

To say that this process was difficult for me would be an understatement. I have never experienced something more challenging than sitting with my supervisor and other interns, reflecting on my internal limitations which are, by their very nature, not visible to me. Yet remaining blind to them kept me from being able to truly be present for the patients. My fear of being rejected if my limitations were exposed kept me from being able to be open, authentic, and vulnerable. We don't have to get into the details but suffice to say that I needed to first learn how to hold empathy for myself before I could offer empathy to others. I had to explore with empathic curiosity my past, my emotions, and my way of seeing the world. I grew over the course of my CPE training, but I am still challenged, at times, to live out the understanding I offered in my final CPE self-assessment:

To show empathy is to identify with another's feelings. It is to emotionally put myself in the place of another. In the midst of another's trauma, this means being willing to be present with them in the void. True empathy for others is difficult and begins with having empathy for myself. In order to enter the void and be fully present for others, I must experience the void in my own life, my conscious and uncon- scious response to trauma, and my coping tools when these responses arise. I must hold space for my own self, free of judgment, so that I can explore meaning and discover a greater awareness. The ability to empa- thize with another is directly dependent on my ability to feel my own feelings, identify them, experience them, and process them.

Empathic Presence

While I have struggled with the empathy needed to enter the void and be fully present with others, my friend and fellow pastor, Rev. Alexis Twito's empathic presence truly has a transformative impact within her community. After the death of Laylah Petersen in November of 2014, The Salvation Army partnered with the Milwaukee Police Department to create a Crisis Chaplaincy Program, to provide support and care to victims of violence and trauma. Pastor Alexis, an ordained pastor in the ELCA, was hired as the first-ever director of the program. She served as Chaplaincy Program Coordinator for five years, until the summer of 2020, when she returned to parish ministry. In her five years as coordinator, Pastor Alexis worked with over a hun- dred volunteer chaplains and they responded to over five hun- dred calls for service in the city of Milwaukee. Here is what she has to say about a defining experience and the overall program:

I pulled my car around the corner from the house and put it in park. And as I grasped the steering wheel before I entered, I whispered a prayer: "please, let me be useful; give me the words to be a comfort." Then I walked into the home where family and friends gathered, weeping, in deep grief over the death of five-year-old Laylah. Our police captain had called me, a local pastor, to come to the aid of this devastated family, reeling from unimaginable loss after a gunman shot up the home and killed this beautiful girl. I was nervous and felt totally out of place and unprepared. What should I do? What should I say? How could I ever bring comfort to this pain? How could I relate? I had no children of my own, I had never lost anyone to random violence. But, as I sat at the foot of Laylah's grandmother, I listened. I listened to her sobs and to her stories. I heard her love and her pain. I held her hand and I cried with her. I was present with her, in the moment, and let her grieve. I gave her the only thing I truly had to give: empathy.

After that morning with Laylah's family, I went on to become the Coordinator of a Crisis Chaplaincy Program that worked with the Milwaukee Police Department to provide support and care to victims of trauma and violence. At the core of our work as chaplains was a simple objective: to show empathy to those who grieved and to help them find the support and resources they needed to move forward. Every day we were called upon to walk into people's grief and trauma, to connect with them, and to help them find comfort, support…hope. Through the warmth of a smile or the gentle touch of a hand upon a back, by wrapping a blanket around cold shoulders or by sharing a bottle of water, our chaplains met people's needs by connecting with their own sense of loss and pain. Our efforts did not erase the grief faced by these families, but hopefully it gave them the strength to face it and move through.

Ubuntu

Ubuntu comes from the Nguni Bantu language which is found in southern Africa. It means "humanity," and is translated as "I am because we are" or "humanity towards others" (Ngomane, 2020). There are moments in which I have struggled with a holistic embrace of humanity, as my judgment sometimes limits my empathy. Through my training in ministry, I have grown and truly seek to continue to reform as I intentionally engage experiences outside of my comfort zone that may lie in my blind spots, which require me to enter the void. Others, like Pastor Alexis and her crisis chaplains, have nurtured their innate skill of empathy and offer it in abundance within their communities by showing up, without judgment, to help where needed. They understand that their individual "I am" is deeply connected to their community's "We are." They understand that true empathy is not simply a feeling shared from afar, but is a presence that calls us into close relationship so that we can all move forward together.

This empathic perspective is also one that I sought to inspire and empower with the children and youth of my congregation.

"I am because we are" extended beyond the walls of our church building. While not entering the grief of a community in the midst of trauma like the crisis chaplains, my youth did enter into the community of our church to engage others with empathetic love. Raising awareness and money for those in need, as they participated in the 30-Hour Famine. Not only serving meals at our local shelter, but sitting with the guests, sharing a meal, listening to their stories, and sharing their own. Our high school youth group went on mission trips – but instead of seeing ourselves as going to do good works and be good Christians, our mission was to connect with the community, build relationships, and offer empathic service. We played soccer with children of immigrant families and we cared for a school garden that needed attention since the students were on summer break. We encountered a lady who turned her backyard into a garden. She invites homeless youth to assist her in the upkeep and then uses the fruits and vegetables produced to prepare a meal for all. We helped out and shared a meal. The challenge I faced, as many faith leaders face, was harnessing the experience of a mission trip and having it reform the hearts of my youth once we were back home. How did my youth's experience change the way they engaged their families, their schools, and their community? Are there ways this empathic perspective can be revealed in our schools? I truly believe that an intentional focus on our shared humanity is key in the reformation, perhaps the transformation, of our school communities.

Reflecting on Your Story

- How would you assess your skills of empathy? How do you express empathy to others?
- What does empathy look like within your classroom? How can you model an empathic curiosity for your students?
- Reflect on your limitations and blind spots. What might stand in your way or arise within you that could prevent an empathic connection with your students?

With their parents? With your colleagues? With your administrations?

♦ What do you believe is the teacher's role in engaging our students' struggles with empathy? Are we called to enter the void to be fully present with our students?

Exploring Our "WHY"

Empathy as a Verb

In his book *Applied Empathy: The New Language of Leadership*, Michael Ventura explores empathy, not as a feeling or philosophy, but as a strategy for understanding oneself and others – exploring empathy "on a personal, communal, and global scale." While his book is written for a purpose of leveraging the power of empathy within a business context, what Ventura offers is powerful for any organization, including the business of school. I am particularly drawn to his exploration and development of seven Empathic Archetypes, the seven faces of empathy.

Vision and Presence

I like balance – and I believe that the success of any collaboration of people needs a balance of perspectives. Not compromise – too often compromise leads to settling on a mediocre middle ground. No, I like balance – passionate voices offering various perspectives. I think Ventura offers this in two faces of empathy, The Cultivator and The Sage. The Cultivator inspires purpose and creates a shared vision. Empathy requires us to understand and work toward our greater WHY. Yet we must strive for more than just a hope-filled vision of success. The Sage keeps us present and in the moment. There is work that needs to be done to bring our vision to fruition. For us to complete this work, as we move forward in our purpose, we must be fully present in the here and now. The fullness of both empathic perspectives is needed for balance.

Holding Space

I love the connection between the archetypes of The Convener and The Confidant. Both embrace the need for space in the nurturing of meaningful, empathic community. The Convener's focus is on the physical space – creating a welcoming place for people to engage and experience one another and the work at hand. Proactive preparation and attentive flexibility allow The Convener to invite people into an empathic space and adapt the space as needed. The Confidant, in a similar manner, holds space for others, emotionally, rather than physically. They create a sense of trust in which empathic listening is practiced. I believe that people like Pastor Alexis reveal these powerful faces of empathy as they offer both physical and emotional space for people in their darkest, most trying of times. I think those of us who connected with the chapter on Intentional Belonging also share a mix of these faces of empathy as we seek to create a space that includes and hold space that affirms each one of our students.

Question, Test, and Venture Forth

I hope we can all connect to at least one of these archetypes, but we all would be well-served to seek growth in all seven. I am seeking to develop myself as the archetype of The Inquirer, as this face of empathy is deeply curious. We must approach people and experiences without judgment. We must ask questions, embrace wonder, and "push for deeper, more authentic truths" (Ventura, 2018). I am working on it. Similarly, The Alchemist is inquisitive, asking questions and testing possible solutions. This archetype understands that there will most likely be failure – but through experimentation, is confident a solution can be discovered. I have included The Seeker with these other two because this face of empathy is boundless, bold, and brave. They are risk-takers and not afraid to experience new things. I like the idea of these three getting into "trouble, good trouble, necessary trouble," as civil rights activist and State Representative John Lewis said (Noxon, 2019). Empathy is often understood as quiet, still, peaceful, and perhaps passive. We are "fully present," "hold space," "create a vision," and "purely listen." Yet, with these final three archetypes, Ventura offers us empathic disruption – in an intentional space that embraces empathy, we can be challenged to be uncomfortable with the status quo, to question the way things have always been, to try unexplored things, to take on new adventures, to fail at times, and to not have all the answers. That is my kind of empathy – intentionally, compassionately disruptive.

We Are One

In an ancient text of the Hindu religion, we are told of a universal joy. *"The one who loves all intensely begins perceiving in all living beings a part of himself. He becomes a lover of all, a part and parcel of the Universal Joy. He flows with the stream of happiness, and is enriched by each soul"* (Drummond, 2008). The more we embrace the shared humanity of all, the happier we are and more enriched are our lives. I believe this – and yet, I think that breaking down the walls that we use to separate ourselves from others is challenging. Children model this universal joy because they still embrace a connection with all people – every new person they meet is their friend. As our students get older, they begin to lose this connection.

Linda Graham, a marriage and family therapist and best-selling author on the subjects of empathy and resilience, which we'll explore in the next chapter, writes about the importance of conscious, compassionate connection in overcoming challenges within our lives (Graham, 2008). As educators, we must foster this connection with our students. We cannot be all seven faces of empathy for them, but we can reflect on our strengths and be willing to offer what we can. In the challenging and too often frustrating work of teaching, it is understandable that there are times our judgment gets the better of us. How many times can a child "forget" their homework? Why don't the parents take more responsibility for their child's behavior? How come the administrators never take the teacher's side? We've all been there. If we are going to develop and demonstrate the power of empathy, we have to take a step back, breathe, and seek "conscious, compassionate connection" with our students, with parents, and with our administrators if our school community is going to successfully overcome the challenges we face. Our school community is one.

Inspiring Our Students' Stories

- ◆ Where do your students feel a conscious, compassionate connection within the school community?
- ◆ How do your students engage one another – with judgment or with curiosity? How can you encourage greater empathic curiosity in their engagement?
- ◆ What exposure to diverse perspectives are available to your students? How can you increase their access to different views and new ways of understanding the world?

Unlocking and Empowering Purpose-Driven Empathy

Beyond the Golden Rule

I know that I started the chapter with the Golden Rule and the sacred text of world religions that speak a similar message. However, while I understand the importance of treating others with empathy, respect, and love, I need to point out a major flaw in the universal belief. You see, the Golden Rule asks us to step back, reflect on our needs, our feelings, and our desires and then offer to others words and actions we ourselves would like to receive. That, however, is not enough and, at times, can be hurtful and possibly harmful.

Think of it like this: Because of my years in sports, I am motivated by coach-like "yelling" as I push myself toward a goal. On the workout app on my phone, I can set the type of voice I want speaking to me while I am working out. I don't choose the motivational speaker voice. My app is set to the drill sergeant voice. I don't need to hear that I am doing well, I want to be challenged to do better. If I assume that all people want to receive feedback in the way I want to receive my workout motivation, I would quickly have children crying, parents angry, and administrators concerned. I cannot do unto others what I want done unto myself. I must stop, listen to what *they* need, reflect on how I am able to serve *their* needs in ways *they* will find helpful and loving. I must, through empathic listening and reflection, do unto others what they have expressed they would like to be done unto them in a way that they feel is beneficial and compassionate.

In school, I think this is most needed in the "What? It's funny" response to "joking around" with others. I get, "Me and my friends do this to each other all the time." As teachers, we need to have our students stop and observe that not everyone thinks it's funny and, most often, the recipient of the "joke" does not find it funny. How you and your friends treat each other is not how you should necessarily treat someone else with whom you do not have the same connection. It doesn't matter if *you* think it's funny – it's not all about you. Empathy will challenge our students to think less about themselves and more about others. As we explored the Key of Focus, we called it being "other focused." Our students must be aware of how their words and actions are received and understood by others. If these things are not contributing in constructive ways to the unity of our classroom, then we must support our students to "do unto others" in a different way.

Embracing Similarities – Exploring Differences

I get what the Golden Rule is saying – there are similarities that unite us all. All people want to feel safe and have their needs met, so make sure your words and actions are not threatening, because *you* want to be able to thrive in a safe environment. All people want to feel part of a community and know they belong, so do not exclude and discriminate because *you* want to be included and respected. All people want their needs and desires valued, so make sure to listen to others, because *you* want your voice to also be heard. Finally, all people want to achieve their goals and live a meaningful life, so do not demean the dreams of others, because *you* want to live a life with purpose. "Do unto others as you would have done unto you" – basic human needs that we must work to ensure for every person.

In Another's Shoes

Theatre is amazing for building one's empathic perspective. Actors seek to become their characters on stage – and this is no easy task. One common acting exercise for building character is to write a backstory. With the information given in the script, what do we know about who this person is? Yet most scripts only give actors the information needed for the specific scene. In Act 1, Scene 3, the character enters the kitchen, takes off his coat, and hangs it on the back of the chair. The given information is pretty simple, but the creation of a backstory adds depth, subtext, and purpose. Where is the character coming from? Is the coat a raincoat, a winter coat, a letterman jacket, or a suit coat? Why does the character hang it on the back of the chair, instead of putting it in the closet – does he live alone so no one cares, is the coat wet and needs to dry, is the closet full of junk so there's no room? You see, theatre and the art of becoming someone else require exploration and curious empathy. Where do you and your character connect – where are you different? Why would your character take actions that seem destructive to oneself or to others? An actor does not need to agree with the words or actions of their character – but in order to take on the role and portray the character with authenticity, an actor must be willing to understand the character's motivation – why is the character who they are? Why does the character do what they do? Why is the character feeling what they are feeling? Artistic empathy.

This artistic empathy can lead to a real-life understanding of empathy. Like characters in a play, our backstory makes us unique. The lived experiences of our students give them varying interests, values, and perspectives. Have students explore the why of each other – make them intentionally stop and reflect on how their own perspective connects the perspective of others. Explain that one person's perspective doesn't have to change yours – and yet, be open to the possibility of change. Let students know that it is OK to disagree. However, it is not OK to be disrespectful or mean when expressing a difference of opinion. Empathy is a skill that I believe our students need to practice every day, in every class, with the support of every teacher because, too often, these differences divide us. When we help our students stop and ask why, we are teaching them an essential step in the empathic connection that can bridge any division.

Empathy as Service

My final suggestion in the exploration of empathy connects to the common practice of community service hours for our students. Does your school require "volunteer service hours"? If your students are like the students I know, then usually they wait until the last minute to think about their hours, then rush to find things they already have done that qualify for "service." Maybe grandma will give you hours because your parents made you shovel her sidewalk. If you give back the money from babysitting your neighbor's kids, will they sign off on "volunteer" hours? I know the forms are due when the teenagers at my church start showing up and asking if they can help usher, be an acolyte, or assist in the childcare room. The end of the school year is always a hectic, but helpful time as these students try to squeeze in service hours.

Are forced service hours really building empathy? Of course, empathy may be an unintended byproduct of these required hours. Certainly, time working in the childcare center offers my youth an eye-opening experience to the challenges of parenthood and raising children. However, I wish the commitment to service was truly voluntary. Perhaps, if not completely voluntary, at least more intentional. Like we explored with the Key of Initiative, how can our students try to "be the helpers" needed within their context? Where in their community do our students see a need with which they can assist? How can our students use their interests and skills to contribute something truly meaningful? I wish an empathic spirit was something we sought to more intentionally develop than require. I believe that it would have a greater impact on our students and within our school community.

References

Drummond, J. (2008). *The Yajur Veda: Taittiriya Sanhita*. A. Berriedale Keith (Trans.). London: Forgotten Books.

Graham, L. (2008). *Mindfulness and Empathy Create Conscious, Compassionate Connection*. Resources for Recovering Resilience. Retrieved 12 November 2021, from https://lindagraham-mft.net/mindfulness-and-empathy-create-conscious-compassionate-connection/.

Krishnamacharya, N. (2012). *The Mahabharata*. Tirupati: Tirumala Tirupati Devasthanams. (Original work published 1983).

New Revised Standard Version. (2009). *Lutheran Study Bible – NRSV*. (Original work published 1989).

Ngomane, M. (2020). *Everyday Ubuntu: Living Better Together, the African Way*. New York: Harper Design.

Noxon, C. (2019). *Good Trouble: Lessons from the Civil Rights Playbook*. New York: Abrams.

Shah, Z. (2018). *A New Publication Launched by the Ahmadiyya Muslim Community: Human Rights Islam Journal*. The Muslim Times. Retrieved 18 November 2021, from https://themuslimtimes.info/2018/06/14/a-new-publication-launched-by-the-ahmadiyya-muslim-community-human-rights-islam-journal/.

Taiqing, L. (2015). *Tai-Shang Kan-Ying P'ien*. D. Suzuki & P. Carus (Trans.). CreateSpace Independent Publishing Platform.

The Analects of Confucius: A Philosophical Translation. (1999). R. Ames & H. Rosemont (Trans.). New York: Ballantine Books.

The Torah: The Five Books of Moses, the New Translation of the Holy Scriptures According to the Traditional Hebrew Text (3rd ed.). (1992). The Jewish Publication Society. (Original work published 1962).

Ventura, M. (2018). *Applied Empathy: The New Language of Leadership*. New York: Atria Paperback.

Wattles, J. (1996). *The Golden Rule*. Oxford: Oxford University Press.

11

The Key of Resilience:
Taking the Path Less Traveled

Connecting to My Story

A Letter from Camp

Dear Mom and Dad,

I can't believe I have been at camp for three weeks already! It's rest period on Tuesday and I'm writing to tell you about the hiking trip I just went on. It was a crazy adventure!

It started last week, before we headed out on our trip on the Superior Hiking Trail. During free time Sunday afternoon, the whole cabin got together to get ready. I would have rather been playing paintball, but I guess it's important to prepare for the trip. In the cabin, we got out our sleeping bags and we laid out the clothes we were going to need for our five-day trip: a second t-shirt and a pair of shorts, a fleece and a pair of hiking pants in case it got cold, raingear in case of bad weather, my baseball cap for the sunny days, and two changes of socks and underwear. I don't know why I needed a change of underwear. I have managed to go this long without changing them. Once our clothes and stuff were packed, our counselors handed out the food we were going to carry in our packs. I got dinner on the last day and was assigned to carry the water pump for filtering our drinking water. I definitely had the heaviest backpack in the whole cabin.

DOI: 10.4324/9781003294634-12

The Key of Resilience ◆ 165

Finally, we reviewed the trip itinerary: drive the camp van up to Egge Lake in Minnesota and then hike to Cascade River State Park – a total of sixty miles!

The next morning, we got up early, filled our water bottles, loaded the van, and were able to get going right after breakfast. Everyone was excited! It was a pretty easy first day – only seven miles from Egge Lake to our campsite at Aspen Knob. Along the way, the bugs were pretty bad. The mosquitoes up in Minnesota are seriously as big as birds – I have like a million mosquito bites! When we got to our campsite, we got to work setting up the tents, collecting firewood, and filtering water needed for making dinner. Everyone did a good job working together as a team. When the sun went down, we stayed up around the campfire telling ghost stories.

The next morning came way too early. At camp we wake up at 7:15am, but on the trail, apparently we get up with the sunrise at 6am. Even though the day before hadn't been too difficult, I was kind of sore. I tried to keep a good attitude, helped with breakfast and clean up, then we set out on a long day, fourteen miles to Dyer's Creek – a solid six hours of hiking. As we made it into Dyer's Creek, I was ready to get the pack off my back. I was sweaty and exhausted, but couldn't just collapse. We needed to get the campsite set up: tents, firewood, water. Even though we didn't want to, I convinced the other guys to help get it done so we could relax. After dinner, we all agreed that going to bed early would be a good idea.

I woke up when my counselor shook our tent: "It's a beautiful day for a Red Arrow hiking trip!" Except, it wasn't a beautiful day – the sky was cloudy and the wind was blowing cold off of Lake Superior. I was really sore and, even after a good night's sleep, I was still pretty tired. Setting out that morning was challenging. We had at least seven hours of hiking ahead of us to get to West Leveaux Pond. Adding to the challenge of a sixteen-mile hike was the gray sky over ahead. About two hours into our hike, the clouds opened and it poured.

Five hours of hiking in the rain *is not fun*! However, since we were prepared, it wasn't as bad as it could have been. I had my raingear, including the cover for my backpack, which kept everything inside dry. The hike was pretty rough, a very muddy trek, but there was a little fun when our counselors let us have a mud fight! Setting up the campsite was hard, finding a dry place to set up the tents was impossible, and collecting wet firewood seemed ridiculous. A couple of guys were in no mood to help out, so I sucked it up and did what had to be done. To say that we had a poor night's sleep would be the understatement of the century! Because of the heavy rains, in the morning, we packed up wet tents and even our sleeping bags were damp. Our counselors decided that we shouldn't try to make a fire, so we ate a cold breakfast of granola bars and fruit. One of my counselors put a whole orange slice in his mouth. He smiled at me with a big orange peel smile. So dumb, but it made me laugh. Still a little hungry, kind of wet, and not very enthusiastic, we all set out on our last full day of hiking – another sixteen-mile hike as we headed to Spruce Creek.

Our fourth day was hard. The weather was pretty nice, but that didn't help most of our attitudes. We all were tired from the long, wet night. We all were hungry from the light breakfast. There was more snapping at each other and even my counselors didn't seem to have patience for our bickering. At one point after lunch, my friend broke down and claimed he couldn't go any further. He was literally crying. I understood how he was feeling, but we had to keep going, so I told him a joke. He laughed, got up, and walked with me. We continued to tell jokes, then I started singing some of the camp songs we all know. At first, it was just me singing, then he joined in, and soon almost the whole cabin was singing as we hiked. It definitely made the hours go by faster and we all made it to Spruce Creek with much higher spirits than when we first set out.

That night's dinner of mac and cheese with chunks of ham tasted like a gourmet feast. Hiking all day made me sooooo hungry! It was so good and I had two big, full bowls. As I got ready for bed, I was thankful that it wasn't raining, I was thankful that I wasn't hungry, and I was thankful that we had made it through the day. Waking up on our fifth and final morning on the trail, I was still pretty tired, but felt better than the day before and only had seven miles to hike that day to Cascade River State

Park. I knew that the day was going to be awesome and we were going to successfully reach the end of our trek. And you know what – it was awesome and we did finish strong!

In my 2-on-1 at the end of last week, my two counselors asked me what I thought about the trip. I told them the truth, that some days were great and other days were kind of horrible. It was definitely the hardest thing I have ever done, but I tried to do my best and was really thankful for the experience. And you know what? On Sunday at the Awards Ceremony, my counselors presented me with the "Best Tripper" emblem. They said that I earned it because of my hard work, my positive attitude, and my great teamwork. I'll show you the emblem when I get home and you can sew it on my kerchief. I can't wait for our canoe trip in two weeks!

OK, the bell is ringing so it's the end of rest period. Oh yeah, send me another toothbrush, I lost mine on the trip! Love you!

Your favorite son,
Dutch

Venturing Beyond the Comfortable

At camp we often speak about the resilient spirit of Red Arrow boys and men for the past one hundred years. In Sunday morning chapel services, a message about overcoming challenges, facing fears, and taking risks in order to grow encourages the campers and counselors to make the most of their time at camp, an experience that is not contained to only the camp property. The RAC experience extends past the cabins in the Quad and beyond the shores of Trout Lake, as campers and counselors venture out to explore the great outdoors on hiking and canoeing trips. While the letter that starts this chapter is fictional, the trip is real and the letter easily could have been written by any one of our campers, any given summer. In fact, the camper's name I chose as the letter's author is to honor our first Trip Director, Dutch Reinhardt, who was part of camp from 1924 to 1989. He knew the importance of building resilience by venturing beyond where we are comfortable, supporting one another in challenging ourselves, and celebrating together when we have overcome the trials of the trail, the rigors of the river, and reached the end of our trip.

Former Red Arrow Trip Director Drew Mueller says this about the importance of our tripping tradition:

Summers at Red Arrow Camp are based on uncommon experiences. Few other opportunities exist for children and teens to leave home for seven weeks, live in a log cabin in the woods, and spend hours each day swimming and boating in a cold, clear lake. Perhaps the most foreign element of camp is the wilderness tripping program, through which each boy is guided on both a backpacking and canoe trip, each lasting three to ten days.

The novelty of wilderness tripping provides an opportunity to teach a variety of skills. Rarely does a boy arrive at Red Arrow his first summer knowing how to paddle a canoe, start a fire, read a map, set up a tent, or tie on a fishhook. Many first-year campers have never spent a night outdoors and fewer have ever traveled to a campsite on foot or by canoe. The idea of carrying everything you need to "survive" for several days on your back or in the bottom of your canoe can be daunting, but learning how to handle uncomfortable situations requires being uncomfortable. Beyond tripping techniques, campers are challenged mentally and emotionally. Hiking or paddling a little bit farther than you thought you could can be strenuous, facing bad weather can be difficult, and being a kind and dependable cabinmate in the midst of stressful situations can be challenging. Yet, pushing onward when you doubt yourself, when you encounter obstacles, when you're upset or frustrated are powerful habits that can only be developed through experience.

After returning home at the end of the summer, few boys paddle a canoe, start a fire, read a map, set up a tent, or tie on a fishhook until they return to camp the following year. Yet they have developed more than wilderness tripping skills. It is their learned ability to accept and overcome challenges that benefits them every day at home and in school, now and as they grow into great men.

Discovering one's resilience and building confidence in that resilience is the foundation of Red Arrow's tripping tradition. Now trips are not simply a challenge for the campers, they can be just as challenging for counselors. Before coming to RAC, at the age of seventeen, I was not the avid outdoorsman that I am today. I had never been hiking or canoeing, I didn't know how to build a campfire, and I certainly couldn't lead children on such adventures. Other than a couple of family vacations, staying at Jellystone campsites, I never had experienced the challenges of nature. Now, after more than a decade of being a cabin counselor, leading two trips a summer, I certainly am no longer scared to face a wilderness adventure – I have a healthy respect for the power of nature, but facing it excites, rather than frightens me. Thanks to my time at camp, I have developed my resilience, knowing that out on the trail and throughout my life, I can overcome any obstacles I encounter, both adventures that I seek out and challenges that are simply part of life.

This resilience has proven essential in my life as I have sought adventure in the great outdoors. Over the years, I have gone whitewater canoeing on some pretty amazing rivers and hiked trails all over the United States. I have skied in the Rockies of Colorado, cycled the bike paths of Oregon, and mountain biked the Northwoods trails of Wisconsin. With one of my Red Arrow brothers, I have trekked to the base camp of Mount Everest in Nepal and have trekked Patagonia in South America. These adventures offered numerous challenges and obstacles.

Outside of adventures that I have chosen to tackle, my resilience has proven strong in the face of life's trials and rigors. Fears and failures, pressure and stress, inequities and injustices have stood in my path, made moving forward seem impossible, and caused me to stumble and, at times, fall. Yet, more often than not, I have been able to rise up, wipe off the mud and the muck, confidently assess the situation, regulate my emotions, and confront life's hardships and struggles. As I have witnessed so many campers grow when faced with the challenges of our camp adventures, I am confident that I have grown as I have faced and overcome the challenges of life's adventure.

Reflecting on Your Story

- ◆ Do you believe challenges (emotional, physical, psychological), like those experienced at camp, are good for children and teens? Why or why not?

- What is the biggest "adventure" you have ever experienced? Can you recall how you felt before, during, and after your adventure?
- What are the biggest fears that you face in your life's journey? Biggest challenges? Do you believe you can face and overcome these obstacles? If not, why? If so, how?

Exploring Our "WHY"

The Adventure of Living

OK, OK – so you are no Grizzly Adams and your students are certainly not from the Swiss Family Robinsons. As Drew says, unless you and your students have opportunities like Red Arrow Camp, you've never had to carry *"everything you need to survive for several days on your back or in the bottom of your canoe."* You can just go to the grocery store. Most of our students simply need to go to their fully stocked refrigerators. Trust me – I know. I taught at a school where ten-year-olds have to wear sport coats. "Swarthy" and "rugged" are not the words I would use to describe any of them. So why explore resilience within your classroom? Fair enough. While our students are not wilderness adventurers, many of our students do not lead comfortable lives. Beyond our classrooms, many students face challenges throughout the school day and outside of school, in their homes and communities. Whether short-term disappointment like earning a low grade on a test or being cut from a sports team, to more ongoing challenges of bullying, peer pressure, or family failures, to systemic injustices involving inequity and discrimination, resilience discovered and developed in our classrooms can empower our students in all aspects of their lives.

Many of us know the alarming research in regards to the mental health of young people. For too many, the "trials and rigors" of life can be deadly. The American Psychological Association reports that the suicide rate has increased thirty-three percent over the last twenty years, with suicide being the second leading cause of death for ten- to thirty-four-year-olds (American Psychological Association, 2014). The Jason Foundation, an organization dedicated to the "prevention of the 'Silent Epidemic' of youth suicide," reports that each day in our nation, there is an average of over three thousand suicide attempts by high school students (The Jason Foundation, 2019). Like I wrote in the chapter about the Key of Enthusiasm, a confident and positive, "Yes, I Can" attitude must be discovered and intentionally developed within our students. Now, I am not making the claim that a resilient perspective is *all* that is needed, but research shows that resilience is an essential piece of this complex puzzle. As educators, we meet students where they are and help them acknowledge and navigate challenging thoughts and feelings so that they can experience hope, peace, and happiness in their lives. We want our students to have the confidence that, even on the hardest days of their journey, they have the strength and support to keep moving forward and make it to the next day and the day after that. As they face hardships and overcome obstacles with our support, our hope can be that they will approach future challenges and struggles with a confident, resilient attitude.

Preparing for Any Path

Proper Preparation Prevents Poor Performance – have you heard of the 5 P's of success? I don't know where I first heard this saying, but it has stuck with me and has definitely been spoken to my campers and students over the years. How are we preparing our students for the challenges that will be faced in our classes, so they can perform at their best? "Proper Preparation" is key. Yet what are we preparing – the child or the path? Too often we seek to make the adventure of learning as easy as possible for our students. We make it so they don't experience failure or we intervene before failure occurs. We offer detailed maps on how to get from point A to point B, and often hold their hands each step of the way. There seems to be a fear that, if we allow our students to stumble and even fall, they might give up on learning and refuse to continue on the journey. Yet the irony is that it is these "protective" strategies that keep our students from discovering and empowering the resilience needed to confidently overcome the inevitable obstacles they will encounter outside of our classrooms. The prepared path within our class may be smooth, but we have failed to prepare our students for life's rocky road.

We were introduced to Dr. Brené Brown back in our exploration of "true belonging." In yet another one of her books, *Dare to Lead*, Dr. Brown makes a statement about parenting that resonated to my very core as an educator and as a camp counselor. She states that parents need to *"prepare their child for the path* by teaching courage, praising effort, and modeling grit, versus trying to *prepare a perfect path for their child* by fixing, praising only results, and intervening" (Brown, 2018, my italics). Teachers need to do the same – prepare our students for the journey, a journey that will have challenges and struggles. Of course, we support and encourage, we empower and celebrate our students, but we must step in less, fix less, and take over less. Our students are capable of far more than we often give them credit for – they can and they will. And when they can't and don't – we can be there to help them reflect, learn, and grow. Our students must face "trials and rigors" within the supportive environment of our classrooms and schools, in order to prepare them for the resilience needed in this adventure we call life.

A Community of Resilience

We are more able to face hardships when we know we're not alone. The American Psychological Association writes: "Many studies show that the primary factor in resilience is having caring and supportive relationships within and outside the family. Relationships that create love and trust, provide role models, and offer encouragement and reassurance help bolster a person's resilience" (American Psychological Association, 2014). As teachers, we can do very little to change the home lives of our students. The reality is that some come from caring and supportive families and communities and, sadly, some do not. Yet our classrooms and the relationships we build with our students can be a source of encouragement and reassurance. When they are with us, we tell them and allow them to demonstrate that they are strong, capable, and resilient – so hopefully, when they are not with us, they will have the right social-emotional "tools" within themselves to confront and overcome any obstacle they encounter and experience the greatness that is inside of them.

In the opening letter, the camper certainly had an internal drive. Yet his counselors supported a resilient outlook: on the rainy days, expressing the beauty of the day, on a cold, wet morning, bringing laughter with a silly smile, and on a rain-soaked trail, taking the time to have some muddy fun. At camp, our counselors certainly become role models for our boys and offer the compassion needed to get through the challenges faced throughout the summer. Our hope is that these campers will then demonstrate the same compassionate support to one another. Earning the Best Tripper emblem is not simply in recognition of one's individual efforts. It requires a camper to demonstrate that he is a strong and dependable cabinmate. Doing what needs to get done when faced with an obstacle is not just about what is best for oneself, it needs to be a sacrificial willingness to do what is best for the whole group: taking the lead to get work done, offering a word of reassurance, helping the other guy out when in need, and lifting the spirits of those around you. We come to the end of our trip together as one cabin. We come to the end of each summer together as one camp family. In school, we must end our time together as one class, one school, one community of learning.

Inspiring Our Students' Stories

- ♦ What are some of the obstacles your students face in your classroom, within the school, within their families, and out in their communities?
- ♦ What are some of the attitudes you see from your students in your classroom? (Determination, Excitement, Apathy, Hope, Frustration)
- ♦ How do your students know/experience your classroom as a safe and supportive environment where they can belong, take risks, and face fears and challenges?

Unlocking and Empowering Purpose-Driven Resilience

Embrace Both–And

Is our role as educators to be defenders or disruptors of our students' comfort zones? Should our learning environments be rooms of bold risk-taking or spaces of solitary sanctuary? There is a common tendency within our culture to see things as being exclusively opposing binary. That is to say, we tend to think of experiences as "either–or" situations. As a teacher, either I am tough or a pushover, either I am caring and understanding or strict and authoritative. Either my class is demanding and challenging, or it is "an easy A" and not taken seriously. When I first started teaching, I bought into this fallacy. I was determined to have Drama be a serious "academic" subject. I went so far as to give written tests on the Elizabethan Age to ten-year-olds and failing grades to "punk" seventh graders who goofed around too much. I sought to prove the educational worth of Drama and demand the respect of the students by making this "Arts Special" as rigorous as the school-labeled "Core Subjects" (Math, Science, English, and History). Yet, just as with the "core subjects," I quickly discovered that standardized assessment and required compliance rarely lead to inspired and passionate learning. I realized that my class didn't have to be either rigorously demanding or overly accommodating, either intentionally challenging or ridiculously fun. My teaching strategy did not have to be "either–or," it could embrace "both–and." In doing so, I could empower resilience through both struggle and support, both challenges and cheers, both obstacles and optimism, and both strategic failure and playful fun.

Rarely, if ever, is life simply two opposing extremes. Nurturing a "both–and" mentality within our classrooms can help our students embrace a resilient perspective in their lives. We must teach students that they can both challenge expectations and still be respectful. They can both disagree with a classmate and collaborate to complete a group project. It's like the power of "yet" in building an enthusiastic attitude; in order to empower resilient success, we must literally remind our students again and again of "both–and." "Mr. Moreno, I don't like theatre." "OK – as you know, you can both dislike the content I am teaching and still understand the need to be an active and enthusiastic learner within my classroom." Boom – mic drop!

The hope in building resilience within our classrooms is that our students can use this Key of Purpose-Driven Learning (PDL) beyond school. They can feel irritated by their parents, sad about a family member's illness, disappointed in a broken promise, or angered by the actions of their siblings, and they can seek to find moments of happiness, peace, empathy, and hope. Encouraging students to choose a "both–and" perspective is not about having them deny their feelings. It is not about having them turn a blind eye to the problems and struggles in their lives and in the world. Rather, we can help them develop a resilient attitude that both openly acknowledges the reality of obstacles and boldly confronts each challenge with confidence and positivity.

Controlled Exposure

Just like with effective curricula, we build, we spiral, we scaffold opportunities for discovering, developing, and demonstrating resilience. At camp, our littlest boys, only seven to eight years old, don't take a five-day trip. They are challenged with a two-night trip, where they hike in and out from camp. They know that the counselors can rather easily get back to camp in the case of an emergency. As the campers gain experience, they go further away for longer periods of time. In fact, the trip described in our opening letter isn't even the most challenging. The Chalet, our second oldest campers, hike for six days on the Isle Royale on Lake Superior and the Chateau, our oldest boys (fifteen–sixteen years old) whitewater canoe in Canada for eleven days. With age and experience come opportunities for greater obstacles and challenges.

The same holds true of my spiraling, middle school Drama curriculum. The ways in which I challenge fifth-graders are different from how I challenge eighth-graders. My expectations at the beginning of each school year are different from my expectations at the end. Every year begins with ensemble-building and trust exercises, in order to build an inclusive and supportive environment in which my students feel a sense of belonging and can confidently take the risk of performing. In fifth grade, students begin their theatrical journey working together in small groups – writing, rehearsing, and performing a number of small ensemble scenes which are performed in front of the class: a fable, a musical theatre dance routine, a Shakespeare fight scene, a conflict-resolution scene. In sixth grade, the students move from ensemble work to the challenge of individual performances in front of their peers: a superhero monologue, a stand-up comedy routine, a Shakespeare monologue, and a dramatic poem. The seventh-grade students return to ensemble work, now focusing on large ensemble collaboration. As a class, the students write and rehearse a one-act play that is performed in the theatre in front of the entire middle school. Finally, in eighth grade, students have a choice from a number of performing Arts electives and can choose how they would like to take on the challenge of public speaking: Improvisation, Musical Theatre Performance, Speech and Debate, One-Act Play, or Poetry Out Loud/Spoken Word. As the students grow in confidence in their abilities, greater resilience can be explored. How does controlled exposure to risk-taking, struggle, and failure look in your classroom from the start of the school year to the end? Are your students more prepared in the fourth quarter to face greater challenges and obstacles than they are in the fall? My colleague would often observe that his students were sixth-graders only for a short while in the middle of the school year, because they came in still fifth-graders and left already becoming seventh-graders. For many teachers, this is a pretty accurate perspective.

Seeking the Pearl in the Muck

"This sucks!" – yup, sometimes life sucks. Having to trek seven hours in the pouring rain on a muddy trail sucks. Preparing an audition for a lead part in the musical and only getting cast in the chorus sucks. Working hard every day for your students, only to get yelled at by an upset parent sucks. Attending yet another staff meeting that could have been an email sucks. Like an oyster in the sea that gets a grain of sand under its "skin," we all face things that irritate and upset us – but we can learn from the oyster who takes that grain of sand and turns it into a pearl. The truth is, life sometimes sucks. Disappointments, frustrations, challenges, and struggles arise. It is never easy and it is rarely fair. Sometimes, the obstacles in our way are the result of our own actions, the consequences of our own mistakes. Many times, the challenges we face are not our fault. They are injustices against us that we endure because we live in a broken world. At times, we can improve our struggles on our own. Other times, we need help because we simply cannot do it alone. We can be angry, frustrated, upset, and appalled – yet giving up or refusing to keep trying doesn't change anything. Complaining, criticizing, and blaming do not make the situation better. We must find a way to make the best of our situation and try to find opportunities that will allow us to grow.

A truth of driven people is that they do not spend much time bemoaning the reality of their present situation. They acknowledge the challenges, set a new path, and get to work trying to overcome the obstacles that are before them. Resilient people know that there is always a pearl to be discovered in the sucky, mucky mess of life. The only way you get to the end of the trail is to keep moving forward, and along the way, there may be a joke to be told or a song to be sung. Working hard in the chorus of the musical shows dedication, reveals true passion, and is an opportunity to improve. Confronting the concerns and fears of parents often strengthens home and school partnerships. Coming out of our individual classrooms and gathering together as a staff can build community and spark collaboration. Keep your head up and your eyes open. Of course, it is difficult to discover a pearl in the muck – but that's why it's a treasure that is so valuable.

And when, after much resilient exploration, a pearl just can't be found – be a pearl creator. That is the greatest achievement of the oyster. It does not simply discover the pearl on the mucky ocean floor; an oyster creates a pearl from the very thing that causes it such irritation. Take the initiative to lift the spirit of the group and offer words of reassurance. Do what needs to be done with pride in your work and a smile on your face. Comfort, listen, empathize, and as challenging as it may be, create a pearl of patience. Actively participate, ask engaging questions, contribute constructive ideas – and when all else fails, bring treats.

Now, I am not saying that we turned a blind eye to inequity or injustice. I am insisting that, in the midst of even the most unjust suffering, a pearl can be created if we come together, work together, grow together, and take a step forward together. Help your students discover the pearls along the paths of their own journeys and empower them to create pearls to be discovered along the paths of others.

Adapt as Needed

Let's make sure we are all on the same page here. I am not offering a one-size-fits-all approach to building resilience. As with all of the Keys of PDL, your educational context matters. I emphasize this now because resilience seems to be the most difficult for many teachers to fully understand and effectively implement. I can't tell you how many times in a workshop or at an Edcamp session, I stress the importance of challenging our students and allowing them to fail, and what participating teachers hear is to let their students drown in an ocean of obstacles without throwing them a lifeline because their suffering will make them tougher. Now, you may not immediately hear the difference between these two perspectives (written with overt sarcasm), so please hear me when I say that you know your students – all of our classrooms and schools are different. Do I believe that *all* students need to be encouraged and supported in expanding the boundaries of their comfort zones – absolutely! Do I believe that every student needs to be thrown up on stage under the spotlight to sing and dance – of course not. Do I believe that every student needs to be sent out into the wilderness for five days to be challenged by the forces of nature – no (although, it would make for an interesting reality TV show). It is my hope that every teacher takes the time to reflect on how they are building a safe and compassionate learning environment, and how, within this supportive community, they are challenging their students, allowing for healthy struggle, and embracing the need for failure as a valuable learning tool in empowering confident resilience.

References

American Psychological Association. (2014). *The Road to Resilience*. Retrieved 18 April 2020, from https://health.usf.edu/medicine/gme/wellness/~/media/0773B749587D479D8217150015E595A2.ashx.

Brown, B. (2018). *Dare to Lead: Brave Work. Tough Conversations. Whole Hearts*. New York: Random House.

The Jason Foundation. (2019). *Facts & Stats*. Retrieved 18 April 2020, from https://jasonfoundation.com/youth-suicide/facts-stats/.

12

The Key of Effort: Being Better Than Before

Connecting to My Story

Living Life with Purpose

One of the most transformative social-emotional learning skills that I experienced as a teenager was the skill of intentional effort. When I was a sophomore in high school, a motivational speaker came to my school for an assembly. She spoke of goals being essential for success. In homeroom, our advisor had all of the students complete the speaker's goal-setting "action step." We wrote down a five-year goal in five areas of life – Relationships, Career, Health, Finance, and Spirituality. I don't remember the speaker's name so, unfortunately, I cannot offer her credit or personally express my gratitude, but nonetheless, her talk and advising "assignment" inspired me. While most, if not all, of my friends probably blew this off – I didn't. I don't really know why, but for whatever reason, I gave it thought and wrote down goals.

From fifteen to twenty, I sought to achieve my goals. Even though I can't remember my goals or whether or not I achieved them, I know it held value because I set new five-year goals from twenty to twenty-five, and I have set goals every five years since. In the past twenty years, my goals have motivated me to train for a triathlon, plan regular "mini-vacations" with my brothers and their families, pay off all my student loans by the time I was

DOI: 10.4324/9781003294634-13

thirty, maintain a prayer journal, and join Twitter in order to be a connected educator. Having five-year goals offered a purpose for my effort. It gave me a direction with which to move – right, left, forward, and even, at times, intentionally backward in order to try a different path.

In my adult life, a defining quality for how I choose to live is with intentionality. My five-year goals help me live into and live out this defining quality. Over the years, I have explored and expanded this intentionality even further, so that I can obtain maximum benefit from my effort. I have made five-day goals seeking to complete the little tasks I always seem to put off. I have made thirty-day goals, as I seek to build new habits, continue to learn, or simply want to take on a challenge. My micro-goals have motivated me to put forth the effort to paint rooms in my home, do one hundred consecutive push-ups, send handwritten notes of gratitude, take on intermittent fasting, and practice my piano and guitar more often. I have found incredible value in seeking to apply intentional effort in all aspects of my life. It helps me when facing a challenging decision, it holds me accountable when I might otherwise make excuses, it motivates me to do what needs to be done, it inspires me to never settle for "good enough," when simply giving a little more effort can ensure that today I accomplished being my very best self.

Motivated to Try

To start the exploration of the Keys of Purpose-Driven Learning (PDL), I shared how Nathan and Lizzie used the cornerstone Key of Confidence to overcome indifference and fear to achieve starring roles in our middle school musicals. To help illustrate the Key of Initiative, I shared the story and the words of one of the most talented middle school actors to come through my program, Connor – and how his willingness to jump in and take risks paid off with many lead roles within his school career and now a promising professional career. Certainly, talent is an important ingredient in one's accomplishments and some of my students used their talents to work hard to find success. However, more than talent, I believe that effort is essential – and Danny's story helps to illustrate this important key.

As I share an honest assessment of Danny's talents and efforts in middle school Drama, please know that we have spoken and he has given me permission to share his story. Danny is a funny guy with a big heart – always has been. He would show up to Drama class with a smile and he put forth the effort needed in class to have successful performances. Danny was never the star – but he always was a dependable chorus member.

You see, it is easy to write about the most talented and high-achieving students, but that certainly was not all of my students. As I write about Danny, know that he represents the vast majority of my students. Good – but in need of more than extrinsic motivation. As you will read in Danny's own words, when he first started in the Drama program, he was only driven by external forces – mainly fear of Mr. Moreno's infamous accountability or the embarrassment of underperforming on stage in front of an audience. Neither force creates an enduring drive. What Danny and so many of my students needed was purpose – a vision of who they could be if they were willing to show up, work hard, and constantly move forward. My Drama program intentionally sought to offer them this goal – a goal of greatness. Yes, standing up on stage, under the spotlights, and hearing the thunderous applause of the audience is a level of greatness some of my students worked for and achieved. Yet, more than that, the goals for all students were a greatness of confidence, dedication, teamwork, and effort. The greatness of each performance was only possible through the greatness of each individual effort and the effort of the ensemble as a whole. While Danny initially struggled with finding the motivation internally, he trusted the process. By the end of middle school, he had experienced the growth that occurs when constant improvement is the goal. He was never a lead. He was never the most talented on stage. Yet he was, and still is, willing to work hard, challenge himself, learn from yesterday in order to make today even better.

During my middle school theatre years, one of Mr. Moreno's guiding mantras was to "be better than your last performance". Looking back, this didn't mean much to me initially because any effort I mustered up was mostly externally driven. Putting effort into memorizing my lines would prevent me from getting called out by Mr. Moreno. Putting effort into learning the dance numbers would make sure that I didn't awkwardly stand out among the other dedicated performers. I initially lacked the intrinsic motivation to improve myself, and this manifested outside of theatre, as well, through a lack of drive to excel in my studies and other aspects of my life. Each day was the same as before with little drive to be better. Working with Mr. Moreno, I eventually did find that intrinsic motivation by looking at all of my "past performances" both in and outside of theatre, realizing that many of them had been staying the same, and striving to put forth the effort to be better.

This intrinsic motivation was shaped out of a desire to stand out and be proud of the person that I was turning into as I transitioned into high school. It's what led me to try a stand-up comedy routine in front of 200 high schoolers on a service trip my freshman year. It's what led me to seek out Mr. Moreno my sophomore year to help me nail the audition for the winter musical, The Mystery of Edwin Drood, as I worked extra hard to nail Durdles' gruff and unreserved personality. It's what led me to run to be one of my school's six esteemed prefects as a senior. This newfound motivation didn't guarantee that I'd succeed: my stand-up routine only got a few laughs, I didn't get the part of Durdles, and I wasn't elected to represent my school. However, this desire to learn from my last performances and put forth the effort to constantly improve has opened many doors for me and still pushes me to be better in everything that I do.

I love Danny's perspective on his time in my middle school Drama program. However, he does sell himself a little short on his effort in those days. Before his comedy routine in high school, he created and delivered his sixth-grade stand-up comedy routine as the Bacon Fairy with confidence and perfect comedic timing: "Bibiddy, bobbity, bacon!" – it still makes me laugh just thinking about it. He did a great job in his seventh-grade One-Act play and the eighth-grade performance elective. He was also one of the eighth-graders allowed to take the Higher Expectation Theatre's high school advanced acting class. By the time he got into eighth grade, he was driven to put forth his best effort not because he achieved stardom in class or on the stage, but because he wanted to keep improving. His honesty about a lack of intrinsic motivation in the beginning years of the program is simply a reality for many of us. Sometimes, it is the external factors that drive our work ethics. However, like Danny discovered, when driven by the intrinsic motivation of self-improvement, the "reward" is a sense of accomplishment as every day you can look back and see the progress you have made. And he has made progress, graduating high school and attending Johns Hopkins University with a major in neuroscience. While in college, he was very successful in a Latin dance troupe all four years and even took on the role of their choreographer in his final years. Having just begun medical school at the University of Virginia, I am sure that the day of his white coat ceremony was a great day. But you know what – I know that he will put forth his best effort each and every day moving forward and even greater days are still in store.

Vertical Effort Vs Horizontal Effort

What Danny experienced at the start of middle school, what many adults experience Monday through Friday for forty hours a week, is that there is always work that needs to be done. We cannot escape it. Whether Danny was extrinsically or intrinsically motivated did not change the fact that he needed to complete the work required in school. Teachers, we know that the same holds true for us. Work that requires some kind of effort is inevitable. The question we need to ask ourselves, we need to ask our students, is whether or not the effort we are putting forth to complete this work is actually helping us grow.

In school, we call it "busywork" – work for work's sake. It drives me crazy as a teacher. Yet, as I look at many of the adults in my life, I see a whole lot of them struggling away with busywork – effort being put in, day in and day out, that, when all is said and done, does very little to improve one's life or the lives of others. I see similar unproductive effort being expected from students every day at school. Are your students being asked to trudge through the muck, to put forth effort, yet make little progress in their development? Whether one trudges ahead or reaches to climb, both require effort. However, at the end of the day, only vertical effort enables them to achieve a new level of growth. Certainly, there are days when all we can do, all our students can do, is horizontally move forward – but when these days turn into weeks and weeks into years, we need to stop and ask ourselves, what is the purpose of exerting all this effort simply to stay at the same level? At the end of the week, the school year, five years from now – how can our students look back and need to look down to see how far they have ascended? Goal-setting, reflection, Purpose-Driven effort, and assessment add intentionality to the work our students are doing and empower them to rise up and experience new heights of achievement.

Better Than Yesterday

We tell our students not to compare themselves to anyone else and I certainly agree. Compare yourself to someone with less, and your pride builds you up for being "better." Compare yourself to some with more, and your shame tears you down for not being "enough." Comparison to others is toxic. But what about comparing ourselves today to who we were yesterday? How can we intentionally make a plan today to be better tomorrow?

In my Drama classroom, our mantra was "be better than your last performance." Students would set a performance goal based on the feedback from their last performance. Throughout the rehearsal process, they would reflect on their efforts as they journeyed toward that goal. Finally, before they would perform, they would ask their peers for specific feedback on their goals. This gave the class more focus and purpose in watching the performance. The audience would then offer the performer feedback, I would add my own observations, and the student would reflect on their performance and the feedback given. My students could observe and articulate how they had improved, where they still could grow, and how their efforts had empowered them to take a step up in their journey to greatness.

Now there is a significant point in this process that I want to emphasize. The students were empowered to define what "better" meant to them. Language matters, as I have said several times throughout this book, so we must be intentional with how we use it. "Better" is a vague word, so it needs to be defined. Each student's "better" is different from the others. One student might need to work on their inflection so they can convey the character's emotions, another might need to move across the stage with more intentional physicality. I had very talented students who defined "better" as taking on challenging accents, creating costumes for their characters, and even building set pieces to enhance their performance. On the other end of the spectrum, I have had students who defined "better" as simply being able to get up in front of the class and this time perform their scene memorized or with eye contact or loud enough to be heard. Beyond my classroom, one student's "better" might require them to put more time into studying. A different student's "better" might require stepping back from perfectionist tendencies that raise anxiety. And another student might seek to be better at socializing and making friends. Because every journey starts in different places, moves at different paces, "better" cannot be a singular, standardized definition created by the teacher and required of all students. For each student, it must be well-defined and articulated so meaningful reflection and feedback can occur, but it must be individual and adaptable to be impactful.

Reflecting on Your Story

- ♦ Have you made goals in your life? Do you find goal-setting to be beneficial? Why or why not?
- ♦ In what situations do you find yourself putting forth your best effort? What are the situations in which you struggled to do your best?
- ♦ Reflecting back on your life, when are times you have worked hard only to trudge a few steps forward? When have you put forth effort and ascended to a new level of growth?
- ♦ How would you define "better" as it connects to your teaching? What can you do today to step up and be a better teacher than yesterday? What goals can you set today to ensure you are a better teacher tomorrow?

Exploring Our "WHY"

Motivating Factors

In his research and writing, Daniel Pink emphasizes that the motivation that drives our effort is not a feeling or a philosophy. Autonomy, mastery, and purpose motivate our effort – the research reveals without question this *fact*. In his book *Drive: The Surprising Truth About What Motivates Us*, Pink makes the argument that the factors which motivate us have been proven time and time again. Yet with all of this research and evidence, there is still a mismatch between what the science shows and what the educational system requires. A solution does not lie in offering a sweeter carrot or threatening with a sharper stick. We must inspire our students in proven, well-researched ways. So many of the Keys of PDL are mistakenly categorized as "feelings" – a feeling of confidence, a feeling of empathy, a feeling of creativity. One of the reasons I like the Key of Effort is that no one ever talks about the feeling of effort. Effort is action – and using the facts of Pink's research we can effectively motivate this action.

Autonomy

I never called the ethos of my Drama classroom a results-oriented work environment (ROWE) – but I was well into creating this type of educational setting when I read Pink's book. This type of work environment gives autonomy to the workers, who are only assessed on the results they produce. Work from home or come into work, work twelve hours a day for three days or work an eight-hour work week – the worker gets to decide. Take breaks when needed, spend time with your family when needed – do what you need to do to be successful and you will be assessed solely on the results of your efforts.

Pink warns that "control leads to compliance..." but advocates that "autonomy leads to engagement" (Pink, 2018). Now, the structure of most schools emphasizes control and much of our teacher training stresses the importance of compliant classroom behavior. My school wasn't much different and my training to be a teacher was pretty traditional. It was challenging for me to believe that offering students full autonomy in "my" classroom would increase engagement and overall learning. But I trusted what the research showed, and every year of my teaching, I sought to release more of my control and give more autonomy to my students. I got to the point in my Drama teaching career when the students moved from a structured program in fifth grade to almost complete autonomy in their eighth-grade electives. They chose what they wanted to perform or created what they wanted to perform. They set their own performance goals, created their own rubrics for assessment, and self-reflected on their performance in order to ensure a stronger performance next time. I observed and offered feedback on what they produced, not just at the end of their performance, but each step along their journey. Were they engaging in quality collaboration in their discussion and rehearsal process? Were they producing challenging goals and effective strategies to meet the goals? Were they producing thought-provoking questions and feedback for their peers? And yes, when the time came to perform, did they produce a theatrical work that they could articulate was "better" than their last performance?

Mastery

Our students do not need grades to motivate their learning. Period. All of the research, including what Pink discovered, supports this truth. It is a fact that I experienced within my gradeless classroom. The moment I got rid of grades, the students actually put forth more effort, their creativity thrived, and their development increased. OK, let's take a step back because I am missing a key step. Once I got rid of the external motivation of grades, the "carrot on the end of a stick" approach, as Pink calls it, I had to offer something else. Not an external reward or threat, but rather a promise of greatness that inspired internal motivation – a commitment of journeying toward mastery together.

Imagine being ten years old, in fifth grade, and after years of seeing the middle school plays and musicals as an elementary school audience member, you are now sitting in the class where it all begins. Mr. Moreno gets up in front of you – a man you have only heard stories about. He stands before you and tells you that within each person lies innate greatness that longs to be discovered. He promises that in your four years together, he will work his hardest to help you develop and share this greatness with the world. He says that together you will confront and overcome one of humanity's greatest fears. He says that it will be challenging, it may be scary, and there will be disappointments – but if you are willing to show up, work hard, and never give up, he promises that you will achieve a level of greatness that no other experience can offer. You know how many fifth graders are willing to fully commit to an epic journey of mastery – all of them.

Purpose

As we near the end of this book, a book that is all about defining the purpose of your classroom, the purpose of your students' learning, I realize that I may have missed one major point. Once you have defined your purpose, please share it with your students. Share it in big and bold ways. Don't simply write in the syllabus and call it a day. It needs to be shared in more than just a letter home to the parents at the beginning of the school year. The purpose of your classroom needs to be declared with enthusiastic intentionality at the start of each school year and in very deliberate ways throughout the year. Please connect your purpose to the purpose of your school and connect the purpose of your school to a meaningful purpose within the world.

Build your students up, give them something to work toward, to be proud of. My fifth graders and their guardians signed a contract in the first week of school at the start of classes and we reviewed it at the start of each year. The contract connected and included them to the grand purpose of the middle school Drama program.

Welcome to Middle School Drama!

Today, we begin an educational experience that will be like nothing you have done before. We are going to undertake a journey to unlock and empower our innate greatness. Every person has powerful skills waiting to be discovered and developed. Every person has a passion that must be awoken and explored. Every person has within them a unique gift that only they can share with the world. Today and each day moving forward, we accept the call to be active participants in the learning, the risk-taking, the resilience that must take place in order for us to become our very best selves. We have four years to accomplish more than we can ever dream possible. I make a commitment to you – I am here, I care, and I will do everything within my power to help each student to find success. Will you make a commitment to our program, to our purpose? Will you show up, put forth your best effort every day, and do everything in your power to succeed and help others find success?

Purpose, a call to action, and a promise of dedication – four years driven to seek greatness. With the time you have with your students, how will you define your purpose in order to motivate commitment, hard work, resilience, and teamwork?

Inspiring Our Students' Stories

- ♦ When do you see your students working their hardest and putting forth their best effort?
- ♦ What do you think motivates your students to try their best? What do you think hinders their willingness to put forth effort?
- ♦ Do your students have goals? How do they make goals, work toward them, and reflect on them?
- ♦ What intentional steps must be taken for you to more fully trust your students with autonomy over their own learning?

Unlocking and Empowering Purpose-Driven Effort

Goal-Based Planning

We all understand the power of goal-setting, right? I don't need to go on and on about the need to set goals in order to give intentionality to our efforts. We know that goals are important, yet we struggle to effectively set them, stay focused on achieving them, and reflect on whether or not we have accomplished them. So, I would like to offer the process that has worked for me that I briefly shared in my story at the opening of the chapter.

I start off with a macro-goal – a big, five-year goal. Five years from now, where do I want to be? In your students' year with you, what can be one of their long-term goals? In their time in middle school, high school, and beyond? A year in the life of a nine-year-old is a big chunk of their life. A five-year goal for a fifteen-year-old is asking them to plan the next quarter of their life. Make the goals big, but specific; have your students record them so they can review them along the way and reflect on them at the end of the allotted time.

For many, macro-goals are a struggle because it is hard to stay driven in their pursuit – we forget, we don't see how today's efforts will impact a goal that is so far in the future. So, I take my macro-goals and I break them into micro-goals – steps that in the coming days, weeks, months, I need to take as I intentionally strive to accomplish my macro-goals. Thirty-day goals are my favorite – a perfect amount of time to stay focused in order to accomplish something substantial and, perhaps, begin to create a habit that will take you even further. Yet we all know that even the most motivated among us struggle and fail, and so the final goal-setting strategy I'll offer is five-day goals. These are very fun to do with your students. On Monday, set a goal that you will accomplish each day that week. This mini-micro goal is a perfect tool for getting something done that you have been putting off. Anytime during the day, your students commit to completing a specific task – read three pages every day, write one page in my journal each night, do ten push-ups each morning when I first get out of bed. Every day you check in with each other and hold each other accountable for the effort being put forth. Completed five-day goals turn into successful thirty-day goals – a book is read, college essays are written, an exercise routine is established. Successful thirty-day goals help in staying motivated and focused on the five-year goals – bills begin to be paid off or savings begin to grow, relationships with family and

Shame-Free Reflection

And we stand at the mountaintop and look back on all that we have accomplished – doesn't that sound wonderful? But – what happens when goals are not met, when our students put forth effort and fail, when, even with their best effort, they forget, lose focus, and fall back into trudging along without purpose? Friends, this happens *all the time*. Please understand that this *is* part of the journey. For all my talk about ascending and accomplishing – forgetting, falling, and failing are just as important to include in the conversation. When I turned thirty, my five-year fitness goal was to train and complete an Ironman triathlon. I worked hard on my running, bought a competitive road bike, and after struggling with my swimming, actually sought training from a swim coach. A year into this goal, it was clear – I did not have the desire or ability to learn to swim 2.4 miles. As I reflected on the fact that swimming would keep me from accomplishing my goal, I decided that I needed to adapt the goal. After all, these are not written in stone. So, instead of an Ironman, I successfully have completed several triathlons that substitute kayaking for swimming – and I love them.

Reflection on our goals is essential in our journey toward achieving them. This reflection must be free of shame and guilt. Neither of these forces are healthy or constructive. OK, your students set goals that they're not achieving – let's explore why. They started off strong, but have lost motivation – how can we re-energize their efforts? A goal made years ago doesn't hold the same meaning – change it, adapt it, or, after thoughtful reflection, maybe let it go. Be honest – and I would encourage you and your students not to give up simply because it is hard or an obstacle has arisen or you have faced disappointment. However, only the goal-setter can honestly reflect on the reason. As teachers, we can push to a point, encourage perseverance in good conscience, and hold our students accountable to what we know they are capable of – but we also need to support a thoughtful change in purpose, respect a mindful decision to focus their efforts elsewhere, and nurture their drive to journey in a new direction. It is a balance that educators face on a daily basis as we seek to help our students be their very best.

An Attitude of Gratitude

Do your students do what is expected of them? Do most of them, most of the time, put forth effort, complete their work, and demonstrate an enthusiasm for learning in your class? I would guess that, for most of us, the answer is yes. Not necessarily all of our students and certainly not all of the time, but most students, most days, are at the least trying to be "good" students. So – when was the last time you thanked them for their involvement, for the impact they have in your classroom? People who feel that they are appreciated – let me correct that, people who know that they are appreciated through the words and actions of others will be more likely to put forth the effort needed to have a positive impact on their future. Sometimes this can be a big honor, like nominating them for "Student of the Month" – but more often, it simply needs to be words of thanks as they are leaving the classroom. Stopping them in the hallway to express appreciation for their participation in class, a kind act you observed, or the quality of the work they turned in. Honor the impact your students are making by letting them know you notice their effort and appreciate their willingness to be their very best.

Reference

Pink, D. (2018). *Drive: The Surprising Truth about What Motivates Us*. Edinburgh: Canongate Books.

13

Empowering Self-Assessment: Exploration and Expression

Connecting to My Story

Just a Phase

I believe that, as an adult, I have a strong sense of who I am, where I have come from, and where I want to go. I would say that I have a healthy understanding of my limitations that might hinder my progress forward, but also a confident awareness of my strengths that assure me that I will find fulfillment in my journey until I successfully reach my final destination. Wouldn't it be great if we all could share this assessment of our individual selves? But I do have to confess something – I did not always feel this way. Perhaps, more accurately, I did not have any awareness of who I was, how I felt, where I wanted to go, why I was doing what I was doing, and if I was ever going to achieve anything. You see, there was a time when I was a teenager.

Anyone who has ever worked with teens, or perhaps you have or currently are raising a teenager, knows that awareness and assessment are *not* their defining characteristics. Now, this isn't a judgment of them, we all were there. It is, quite honestly, very developmentally appropriate for teens to be – what's the word I am looking for? Clueless. After working with teens for so long, I often apologize to my mother for ever having put her through that stage in my life.

DOI: 10.4324/9781003294634-14

My brothers and I were knuckleheads. True, we were academically gifted and reasonably well-behaved, but we were knuckleheads. Parenting us was often a routine of asking us why – Why are the sleeves ripped off all of your t-shirts? "I don't know." Why are all of the bikes taken apart? "I don't know." Why is only half the lawn mowed? "I don't know." Why is your math teacher calling home? "I don't know." Why is your best friend mad at you? "I don't know." So many questions, all with the same response. Now certainly, there were times that we knew and chose not to answer in order to avoid getting in trouble. But a lot of the time, I believe we really didn't know. We didn't take the time to consider the consequences of or reflect on our actions. I love my mom and think she is a great parent, but her response was never, "Interesting, let's explore your WHY, so we can raise your self-awareness and perhaps encourage more constructive actions in the future." It just wasn't the parenting style in the '90s.

Do as I Say

Often schools are not much better than '90s parenting when it comes to addressing the self-awareness and self-assessment of their students. Schools dictate expectations, and when those expectations are not met, consequences are carried out without much discussion: absent without a doctor's notice – it goes on your record; late to class – written up; goofing around – scolded; missing homework – recess detention; perform poorly on a test – failing grade. Too often, we forget to ask why our students are doing the things that they are doing or we assume we know the answer.

Now, I started down the path of school discipline when addressing the opportunities we offer students to explore their WHY, but often teachers miss opportunities to raise students' awareness within their classroom, even when it's not connected to challenging behavior. Teachers tell students where to sit, what to study, how to complete a project, when to turn in their work, and who they should collaborate with when completing an assignment. As a substitute teacher, I see it all the time. Teachers, working with students of all ages, telling students exactly what to do in order to get an "A" in the class. The only question they ever ask is "What do I have to do to get an A?" The answer students give to the "why" of their learning becomes a repetitive "Because that's what I was told to do to get an A." Getting an "A" becomes the purpose of school. No awareness, no freedom of expression, no exploration of the unknown, and no authentic assessment of their learning. Many classrooms dictate the learning process and only assess compliance and completion, expressed with a letter, a number, or a percentage.

The first and most important step, I believe, any teacher must take when seeking to empower their students with the abilities to effectively self-assess their own learning is to remove the focus from grades. I understand that this is an incredibly challenging task, as our students' learning is entrenched within a system of grading. However, if our students are only concerned with getting an "A," they cannot meaningfully explore or express their learning journey.

Something's Simply Gotta Go

While not the purpose of school, nor the focus of learning, I understand the importance of content knowledge as the means by which we explore social-emotional learning (SEL) and I recognize testing as one of the tools with which to demonstrate these skills. However, in my experience, the same importance and recognition cannot be extended to grades. You may not agree with me, but I want to make my stance clear. I believe that grading, at its best, is an antiquated form of passive assessment that provides little to no authentic or constructive feedback to students. At its worst, grades are actively harmful to the purpose of developing and empowering our students' passion for learning (Kohn, 1999). I make the bold claim that a drive for learning is innate, within all of our students – and yet, for many teachers, this is not what we experience in and from our students. Unfortunately, schools, the very institutions that we believe should inspire and nurture learning, utilize destructive grading strategies that crush motivation, destroy drive, and extinguish passion in and for learning. A bit dramatic, perhaps – after all, I am a theatre teacher. Yet I do not believe that I am wrong.

I know, I know – for almost all of my readers, throwing out grades is simply not an option. Your school and your district require grades. Fine. So here is my suggestion – stop spending so much of your time and energy on grades. Take time to thoughtfully consider shifting your efforts from grading to empowering your students to assess themselves, their learning, and their contribution to the purpose of your classroom.

Articulating Leads to Internalizing

If I am going to challenge you to shift your focus away from grades, I must give you a new language to use. With the Keys of Purpose-Driven Learning (PDL), we have been given the language with which to engage our students and their development. The language of grades is something we encounter, is something our students encounter, almost every day of school for the vast majority of time in formal education. Changing our language will certainly not be easy. I have been using this language for years and still find myself praising my niece for earning straight A's on her report card or asking my nephew what he scored on his math test. The shift in language will not happen overnight – and yet, with consistency and intentionality, teachers can effectively model the use of this language. The more teachers use this language, the more the students will use it. The more the students use it, the more they internalize it and begin to become aware of these skills in their learning.

Practice, practice, practice this language. Remove grade-based language and practice PDL language. Instead of encouraging students to work together to get a better grade – remind them that their classmates are depending on them to contribute to the group. Instead of asking students to revise their paper for a higher grade – express that taking the initiative to revise offers them the opportunity to demonstrate their best effort. Students shouldn't participate for a grade. Acknowledge the confidence that is needed to raise one's hand and contribute an answer. Show appreciation for the empathy a student has for another or the effort shown in completing an assignment. Praise both focus and enthusiasm when students demonstrate these skills at constructive times and encourage these skills when they are lacking within the classroom. You see, these are more than just words. This is more than just language. The Keys of PDL are skills needed for learning. Before we can work with our students in building these skills, they must know what they are, that they exist, and that they are innate. Our students come with these skills, undeveloped perhaps, but within them – one of our first steps is helping them discover them. Once aware of these essential skills, we can work together to develop them.

It's All Connected

I don't know if you have noticed, but throughout this book, it has been difficult to only address one aspect of PDL or just one Key of PDL. Very quickly you and your students will discover what makes writing a book like this so challenging – all of these skills are interconnected. True belonging is rooted in a confidence in your authentic self. Putting forth your best effort takes initiative. Demonstrating that you are a dependable teammate requires a commitment to and focus on completing the needed work. Empathy is a combination of curiosity and compassion. Enthusiasm and creative solution-seeking in the face of an obstacle are essential aspects of a resilient spirit.

What is so fun about the exploration and expression of these SEL skills is that no two people see them in the exact same way, because no two people experience them in the same way. It is the way self-assessment becomes an integral part of the Purpose-Driven process. What I observe as confidence, the students might express as resilience. What a classmate might experience as a struggle with dependability might be assessed by the student as a struggle with focus. What I might assess as a lack of enthusiasm and effort might be expressed by the student as a fear of not belonging and being affirmed. The interconnectedness that makes the exploration of our SEL so dynamic and intriguing requires that the expression and assessment of these SEL skills be empowered within each individual student.

Self-Assessment

We do not only unlock and empower these skills – just as important, we must help our students reflect on their development, articulate their growth, and assess the overall learning with this Purpose-Driven perspective and language. Self-assessment is challenging, no doubt about it. So it is always funny to me when teachers give it a try without the proper preparation and training of their students. If you invite students, who have never been asked to self-assess before, to think about how they are doing in class – they are most likely going to give one of two answers. Our middle and high school students will respond with the standard teenage, "I don't know." While elementary-aged children and our high-achieving students will assess that they are doing great. I mean, "great" is the right answer when getting an "A" is the goal – right? When students are asked for the first time to assess and articulate their learning, it is a challenge because they most likely have never done it – so they truly don't know or simply will give the answer that benefits them the most. Shifting this mindset is not easy and takes intentional time and energy.

Assessing the Stories We've Heard

Instead of sharing with you a new story from one of my students, campers, or youth group members about the importance of self-assessment, I think it is valuable to simply look back at the stories already told in previous chapters. Yet, instead of reading it as an exploration of the Key of PDL which was being addressed, let's look at the stories through the lens of self-assessment.

We started with Brittany, as she assessed the sense of belonging she felt within the youth ministry program at church. More than just an assessment of the ministry, Brittany expresses the internal value she feels, saying *"I know that I am loved just the way I am and I am thankful to have a place where I belonged."* This is what Brené Brown explores in her definition of true belonging – an internalized confidence that allows a person to share with the world their authentic self. Brittany's self-assessment reveals this confident sense of true belonging.

In self-assessing how his involvement in theatre helped his ability to confidently take risks, Nathan writes that *"[Theatre] helped me to realize that confidence doesn't equate to always having the right answer, but rather being able to trust my ability to attempt problems with imperfect solutions."* Richie offered a self-assessment of his challenges as an ADHD child in classes where he was expected to sit still and remain quiet: *"I struggled to focus in these classes because of this environment, and it would affect my ability to learn the subject at hand."*

As young adults, Connor and Danny assessed how their social-emotional development in theatre currently helps them work hard and move forward. Connor wrote, *"I have a dream, a plan, goals. But I was never going to find out what lay ahead on my journey simply by dreaming…I needed to take the initiative to move forward on my journey."* Danny expressed that his *"desire to learn from my last performances and put forth the effort to constantly improve has opened many doors for me and still pushes me to be better in everything that I do."* It makes me proud that the assessment of their middle school learning reflects a lifelong impact.

Lizzie's self-assessment of her confidence is probably my favorite, because it comes from a letter she wrote in sixth grade. I am thankful that these other young adults are able to look back and see the value in the development of their social-emotional skills, but I think it is pretty neat that there is written proof that Lizzie was able to assess her growth in the moment at the age of twelve: *"Last year my comfort zone didn't want to budge, but this year I feel that it has leaped a whole foot into new and exciting things I have yet to experience."*

I am filled with pride that the young people I have worked with over the years are able to self-assess and articulate their growth as it connects to their social-emotional well-being. Through the intentional strategies of PDL, I know that your students can explore and express the impact of their learning, as well.

Reflecting on Your Story

- ♦ When you were a student in school, did you have the opportunity to explore and express your own learning? If so, how has that impacted your perspective? If not, how did the assessment from your teachers influence your development?

Empowering Self-Assessment ◆ 201

- In your adult life, do you reflect on your past experiences, your limitations and strengths, and your goals for the future? How do you believe this intentional awareness and assessment can help you grow as a person?
- How can you make intentional changes in your planning, teaching, and feedback to shift the focus of your classroom from content, testing, and grades to the discovery, development, and demonstration of holistic learning?

Exploring Our "WHY"

Social-Emotional Learning Competencies

I introduced you to The Collaborative for Academic, Social, and Emotional Learning (CASEL) and their definition of SEL way back in the first chapter. Now, here we are learning about the transformative power of self-assessment and they have more to offer us. Their Five Competencies are a perfect framework to support our exploration of PDL within our classroom, as we seek to ensure the holistic development of our students (CASEL, 2020).

Inside-Out: Self-Awareness and Self-Management

When working with my students, I like to begin exploring SEL by unlocking within before empowering beyond oneself. I work with a wide range of ages, yet no matter the age, doubt and fear are challenges we all face. As we make the inevitable mistakes that come along with learning, the reaction of blaming others, the refusal to take ownership of words and actions, and the desire to point out the failing of others are go-to defense mechanisms for many of us. I want my students to embrace our full range of emotions. When challenged, I want them to take a deep breath, step back, and reflect on their own feelings, words, and actions. The language of PDL supports this objective. Helping students develop their confidence allows them to celebrate their value and believe in their worth even when mistakes are made. Students who are resilient are more willing to confront their limitations and consider how they might work to overcome self-inflicted obstacles. Creativity and curiosity empower students to explore the unknown that is within them, identify and embrace their emotions as they arise, and ask questions that reveal a deeper understanding of who they are and who they want to become.

With greater self-awareness, students can begin the process of regulating their emotions and managing their words and actions. Students can take the initiative to use their inner focus to reflect on instead of reacting to situations as they occur. They put forth the effort to stand up for what they believe and share their thoughts in effective ways, and yet are willing to do the hard work of responding with empathy when others share a contrary point of view. And, even in difficult situations, I want my students to maintain a positive perspective and an enthusiastic attitude – even when life is hard, life is worth living!

Express Yourself: Social Awareness and Relationship Skills

While clearly essential in self-awareness and self-management, PDL is needed and used within the relationships our students build, as well. As we seek to create a space of inclusion and affirmation, in which our students might experience true belonging, we need them to intentionally develop social awareness. The external keys of empathy, dependability, and "other focus" are emphasized in building and maintaining meaningful and lasting connections. I want my students to truly consider how others feel. I want them to always take into consideration the perspectives of others and understand that often they are different than their own. I want them to understand and accept that everything is not always about them – at times, self-sacrifice is needed for the communal well-being. I want them to feel safe, affirmed, and included, but I also need them to be active participants in ensuring others feel the same sense of belonging. In my classroom and up on stage, I want my students to do what they say, honor their promises, and demonstrate trustworthiness. And when they mess up, I want them to admit their mistakes, apologize, and work to restore the relationships that add value to their lives.

Empowering Self-Assessment ◆ 203

Remember to Make Good Choices: Responsible Decision-Making

If you are paying attention, you may have noticed that Belonging and all ten Keys of PDL have been connected to the first four competencies. However, I am going to double-dip with several of them as we explore the competency of responsible decision-making. I have a lot of teens in my life, and one of my favorite things to say to them whenever they are going out with their friends is to "Make Good Choices."

At first, it is often met with defensiveness, as if I don't trust them to make good choices and constantly need to remind them – but after a conversation about the need for teens to be constantly reminded, they accept my reminder. From then on, "make good choices" is usually met with "I'll try." This, of course, is answered with Master Yoda's famous words, "Do or do not. There is no try." Gosh, I love working with teens!

But in all seriousness, PDL offers powerful language when exploring and expressing responsible decision-making. We want our kids to analyze the choice in front of them with curiosity. We want them to focus on the positive and negative outcomes before jumping to a decision. We want them to take the initiative to communicate their decision to the right people before taking action, demonstrating that they are dependable. And if – no, when – they happen to make an irresponsible decision, we want them to confidently confess their mistake and express empathy for those impacted by their decision. The same self-assessment that we are seeking to empower in their learning will be empowered in the assessment of their words and actions beyond our classrooms.

Inspiring Our Students' Stories

- ◆ Where in your students' lives do you see they have the opportunity to explore and express their own opinions on their growth and development?
- ◆ Do you trust that with preparation, practice, and patience your students will be able to effectively reflect on and assess their own learning? Why or why not?

- How might empowering your students' ability to authentically self-assess impact their lives outside of school?

Unlocking and Empowering Purpose-Driven Assessment

Put the Focus on You

The art of reflection requires practice. At the start of the journey of preparing your students to assess their learning, let them practice on you. As an exit ticket at the end of class, have them assess your teaching, the strategies used to cover the content, the techniques used to manage behavior, the SEL language you used and encouraged. In a journal entry or as part of a class discussion have your students contribute their observation of your use of SEL in and through your teaching. If you intentionally offer an SEL expression that they miss or don't assess, you can address it as a teachable moment. Did you offer ways in which each student had the opportunity to confidently participate? Did you offer the content in an engaging and enthusiastic manner? Did you allow the students to take breaks when they began to lose focus? How did you demonstrate resilience and adaptability when the lesson didn't go as planned?

Intentionally introduce PDL to your students, let them know that you are trying to model the SEL exploration and expression that you hope they will demonstrate, then invite them to actively observe your practice in class and allow them to offer constructive feedback. It is true that the older the students are, the more likely it is that they will be trying to "catch" you using old language of grading or missing an opportunity to express awareness – however, even in your struggles with mastering an SEL demonstration, you are empowering your students' SEL awareness and articulation.

Shift the Focus to Them

With a few "teacher-centered" opportunities to assess completed, I encourage you to offer opportunities for your students to assess themselves. Start by offering reflection questions that are open-ended and require them to use Purpose-Driven language. How are you demonstrating dependability as a member of your group project? Today several students struggled with the lesson, how might you show empathy for them? Instead of taking a test, how can you creatively demonstrate your understanding of the content?

No questions about grades – rather, questions that place the awareness on how they can develop and demonstrate key SEL skills. I have experienced it over and over again – after a few "required" assessments, students will begin to use this language on their own and in their expression of their learning. The language of PDL will show up in a journal reflection, on a lab report, and within an email exchange. Students do this, not because these are some kind of magical words, but because it feels good, it feels meaningful, it feels powerful to be able to articulate one's learning in a way that expresses vulnerable struggle, impactful growth, and holistic learning.

Rubric-Less Learning

At this point in my book, my advice might feel repetitive – and for that I am sorry, but the key to unlocking and empowering our students' fullest potential lies in us turning their learning over to them. So give up control, give fewer instructions, get rid of rubrics – OK, maybe you don't have to get rid of them, but let the students create them. Let them have a say in the growth they are trying to achieve, how they would like to demonstrate their learning, and what aspects of their demonstration they would like specific feedback on. Certainly, there are specific standards and objectives that must be assessed. I would challenge you to let the students decide how and when these benchmarks are demonstrated.

Besides the demonstration of the Keys of PDL, my Drama students had to demonstrate certain writing skills with their scripts, acting skills in their performances, and collaboration skills in their ensemble work. Over their time in my program, these students were empowered to decide when and how these skills were assessed. This added intentionality to their planning and gave purpose to the demonstration of their learning. And you better believe, in the self-assessment of their theatre skills, they used PDL language.

Articulating the Learning

So how do we defend the grade? Yuck – what a horrible question. How can we articulate our students' learning – much better. The wonderful thing about empowering our students' self-assessment is that teachers don't have to struggle to come up with things to say. The students put forth the effort to articulate and assess their learning and we simply need to respond. It is so much easier to respond with meaningful feedback to a self-assessment than to create an assessment for a student from scratch.

Self-assessment also makes student–teacher meetings so much more Purpose-Driven. If you agree with the student's self-assessment, you can offer positive feedback on their SEL awareness. If you don't agree, then without invoking shame, you can ask the student how they came to their assessment. "I am curious" or "I wonder if you could share with me an example of these SEL skills you assessed in your work or in class?" While your observation is usually correct, I will admit to missing expressions of learning that students share in our one-on-ones which have changed my feedback for them. On the other side of that coin, I would have students assess themselves more "harshly" than I would. Feedback then becomes a way of sharing what you observed and seeking to strengthen their confidence in and awareness of their growth. Quality and meaningful feedback based on your students' assessment of their own learning.

Outside Observations

Do you know how impressed parents, guardians, and administrators are when you can offer insightful student assessment – not in your words, but in the words of the student? It also ends parents' and guardians' questioning of the assessment before it even begins – this is what your child says. Now, when the student assessment and teacher feedback are not aligned, it can be challenging – but again, the focus can stay on how the student needs to articulate their process for reaching their assessment. Keep the focus on the student's learning.

A parent asks about the grade you are required to give – turn the question back to the learning. "What aspect of your child's learning would you like to know about?" "Here is what your child says about their learning." When students are trained to articulate their learning and asked to assess their limitations and strength, they will. And what they express will help you in your conversations with anyone looking to question or challenge the learning within your classroom.

References

CASEL. (2020). *What Is the CASEL Framework?* Retrieved 28 March 2021, from https://casel.org/fundamentals-of-sel/what-is-the-casel-framework/.

Kohn, A. (1999). *From Degrading to De-Grading*. Retrieved 1 December 2021, from www.alfiekohn.org/article/degrading-de-grading/.

Conclusion: A New Story of Learning

The Same Old Story

The Way It's Always Been

Building an inclusive classroom is wonderful – but how does it help our students learn their multiplication tables or understand chemical bonds? So educators prioritize teaching their content, covering everything within their grade-level curriculum and classroom textbook. Using the Keys of Purpose-Driven Learning (PDL) when speaking with students and parents sounds great – but how does it help our students score well on state-testing and their AP exams? So teachers focus on preparing students to take standardized tests. Allowing our students the space and voice to explore and express their challenges and strengths can have a meaningful impact on their learning – but how is that impact quantified in a grade? There are no metrics for expression of empathy or enthusiasm and no benchmarks for the proficient demonstration in creativity or curiosity, so teachers simply give a grade.

I hear the skeptics and the nay-sayers – sure, an intentional focus on belonging, social-emotional learning (SEL), and self-assessment sounds nice, but how can we dedicate precious time to inclusion and well-being and still cover the needed content?

How can we evaluate the Keys of PDL on a scantron test? How can we prove our students' assessments fulfill the state and national standards? The educators who ask these questions cling to the teaching techniques they experience when growing up and the ways they were instructed to teach in their college training. They are not questioned by parents because it is the way many of our students' parents were taught when they were in school. And often these teachers have the support of their administrators because adherence to the traditional status quo will always be less disruptive and more compliant.

The unknown is always scary. The unexplored is always challenging. The innovative is always disruptive. However, for the sake of our students, we need to boldly let go of the old and embrace the possibility of the new. In the opening chapter of this book, I asked about your story – the experiences that shaped your identity, your life choices, and your passion. I asked you to reflect on the story you wish to write as you journey forward – your goals, your mission, your purpose. Throughout this book, I have asked you to reflect on your own story of learning – about your time in school. What content knowledge did you retain? How did testing prepare you for the real world? What impact do your grades have on your life now as an adult? How have the traditional systems and structures of school unlocked your passion for learning and empowered your mental health and social-emotional well-being? My friends, we know the answers – most of our stories of learning have not been inspirational, dynamic, or intentional. Many of our goals, as teachers, speak of making an impact in our students' lives. What can we take away from our stories of traditional learning in order to empower our students to write stories of greater inspiration, passion, and purpose?

Hindsight Is 20/20 – or so They Say

I did very well in school. With the exception of a short-lived, junior high "punk" phase, I was a very good student, and even through those middle school years, I was academically strong. In high school, I was in honors and AP classes, excelled in my coursework, and was inducted into the National Honors

Society. I knew the content of my classes and could demonstrate that knowledge through the required assessments – projects, papers, and so many tests. In school, I would have told you that I "learned" a lot, which was evident in my high GPA and my scores on the ACT and SAT tests. Yet, for all that I claim to have learned, decades past high school, I would now struggle to tell you very many facts about the Peloponnesian War or the Revolutionary War or even *The Pushcart War*. Helping high school students with their Pre-Cal or even my middle school students with Algebra work when I substitute is definitely a challenge. And sad to say that, after four years of French, these days, I can say little more than hello. *C'est vrai!* If we are honest, for most of us, the vast majority of content knowledge we "learned" in school has long since been forgotten. Facts, dates, names, and vocabulary on which we were so heavily tested have failed to remain important in our daily lives. The grades for which we worked so hard, that caused so much stress, that defined who we were as students for so much of our formal education – well, what do they matter now? All of my "A's" did not prepare me for the challenges of life. If the content we were taught has not lasted, if the tests we passed no longer matter, if good grades in the real world have no meaningful impact – what did we learn in school? In hindsight, how do we answer the question – what was the purpose of school in our lives?

For me, I remember the **curiosity** needed to build a marble roller coaster in Physics and the **focus** required to tackle the challenging problem-solving of Trig. I recall the **confidence** needed to get up in front of the entire middle school as Elvis in our all-school musical production. I remember the **creativity** required to help my grade-school teacher decorate our classroom windows and needed to create my AP Art portfolio. From fifth to twelfth grade, I grew by putting forth my best **effort** every day at practice as the quarterback on my football team. In band, I practiced my trumpet just as hard to demonstrate my **dependability** to my director and fellow musicians. Losing every wrestling match from first to fifth grade developed the **resilience** I needed to make it to the State Tournament when I was in high school. I remember the ridiculous **enthusiasm** of our men's choir which offered a needed break from the rigors of school, as we interrupted classes to sing doo-wop love songs on Valentine's Day. Taking the **initiative** to serve within my community as a Cub Scout and then as a member of Key Club allowed me to learn the importance of **empathy**.

Perhaps it is similar for you – it is not the content, testing, or grades that I remember and value from my days in school, but rather it is the life skills, the "soft" skills, the employable skills, the PDL skills. Yet I was well into my adult life before I was aware of this impact, before I had discovered the language with which to speak about my limitations and strengths, and before I made a connection between these skills and my lived experiences. In school, I did not have the opportunity to explore and express who I was and how I learned. Of course, back then, I probably would not want to have shared my authentic self because school was not a place where I experienced true belonging. My story involved parents, teachers, and coaches dictating my identity, feeding me my learning, and merely requiring me to obediently regurgitate it for a passing grade. I was "good" at school, so I never thought of challenging the story I was being told. As I have written the story of my learning since my formal education, I am thankful that my journey has offered me a sense of belonging, the language with which to reflect on my holistic well-being, and the confidence to assess myself honestly and with openness to the feedback of others. However, I don't want the young people in my life to have to wait until adulthood to begin writing their story of being Purpose-Driven. I want them to experience it today, so they can write a story of greatness now.

A New Story of Learning

Many of the stories from our time in school, the stories of learning of parents and teachers, focus on content, testing, and grades. That's what we were told learning was. What if we empower our students to write stories that focus on the discovery, development, and demonstration of the key SEL skills that lead them on a journey of greatness within our class, each day of school.

Science becomes more than following a series of steps in a lab to prove a hypothesis. It is a story about developing a **curiosity** for the unknown and having students ask "why" until they reach a conclusion. Math is not about showing your work and getting the right answer. It is about building **resilience** when encountering a problem one doesn't understand. Language Arts become more than reading a bunch of chapters in a book and writing a summary that is grammatically correct. It becomes a story of our students striving to be **dependable** members of the class, who do their work so they can take the **initiative** to boldly share their voice and perspective. History is more than memorizing dates, places, and names. It is about connecting with the past to build **empathy** with the decisions of historical figures, the struggles of soldiers in battle, or the fight of slaves for freedom. We want our students to have positive, **enthusiastic** attitudes, even when engaging a part of their story that is disappointing, frustrating, or difficult. We want to encourage students to put forth their best **effort** every day and **focus** on using content knowledge for their own personal growth, within their relationships with others, and in their contribution to the world. We strive to develop students who are **confident** in their ability to learn whatever content is presented to them, and who share their thoughts and opinions regarding the content without fear of failure. We need students whose **creativity** enables them to engage and apply the content in innovative ways as creative solution-seekers. Now that is a story for our students worth writing and sharing with the world.

Here I Stand – I Cannot Do Otherwise

Let's intentionally rethink, redefine, relearn how to discover and develop a love of learning: student-driven rather than teacher-dictated, passion-driven rather than grade-focused, Purpose-Driven rather than system-standardized. Three years into my teaching, after hearing Tony Wagner speak about his book *Creating Innovators*, I made dramatic changes to my Drama classroom. These changes, explored throughout the book, made my teaching and my classroom "look" very different from other teachers. I was questioned on more than one occasion by parents, other teachers, and administrators about my "non-traditional" approach, about the students' learning, about "best practices," and about my "proof" that PDL was an effective pedagogy. It will never cease to amaze me that even though people will openly admit to being part of a failing traditional system, they will seek to tear apart a new process, they will ignore the limitations of the system they are in, and they will resist trying something different and braving the unknown.

With little support in those early years, I had to trust myself as a professional – standing firm in what I knew through my studies, through my independent exploration, through my experiences working with young people in and out of a formal classroom setting, and through my relationships with my students. I think that deserves repeating – *I needed to stand firm in what I knew as a teaching professional*. I know what my students need, I know how my students thrive, and I know how I can support them in their learning and growth. Long before completing extensive research to "validate" PDL, I knew the impact of my Purpose-Driven classroom because I knew my students through the strong relationships I built with them. Teachers – please, hear this, you know your students. Confidently and intentionally embrace what you know to be true – you are the trained professional. With this confidence and humility, boldly explore what needs to intentionally change in your classroom in order to more fully connect, inspire, and empower your students' learning.

Here is what I know to be true with my students within my context: Exploration occurs more through creative play rather than required work, more through Socratic discussion rather than teacher-led lecture, more through project-based demonstrations of learning rather than traditional and standardized testing, more through self-reflection and constructive feedback rather than grade-based assessment. This does not mean the latter is never utilized, but rather, in my classroom, the former is intentionally emphasized and prioritized in order to lead to self-discovery and communal engagement.

I know that learning is not contained to traditional classrooms. Students learn on the sports fields and courts, in the music room and on the auditorium stage. Students learn at home, within their communities, and in their experiences beyond their communities. I know that truly successful people never stop learning. Far too many people think their "learning" ended when they completed high school, college, or trade school. Far too often, we try to contain learning to the confines of the years of formal education. I know that learning is a life-long process, that we are *all* learners. I toyed with the idea of calling this pedagogy Purpose-Driven *Teaching* or define it as a Purpose-Driven *Classroom* – and while I believe that *all* people can teach one another regardless of age, the power lies in an intentional openness to learn from one another. Learning is an opportunity that is not restricted by our age, or our titles, or our location – young or old, student, parent, teacher, or adminis-trator, in school or at home – learning is limitless.

I know that authentic learning cannot be required, it needs to be inspired – and I know that inspiration comes from those with whom we have meaningful connections. I know that learning is all about relationships and I have experienced how building an honest and open relationship with young people can profoundly impact our lives. Folks talk a big game about the importance of the relationships between teachers and students; yet, when push comes to shove, there is a traditional hierarchy that supports an imbalance of power. I know that the student–teacher relation-ship can make a lasting impact when we move past the trad-itionally defined roles of student and teacher. This means that on our journey, my experience and expertise as the "teacher" is simply one person's contribution to our overall learning experi-ence. Yes, my contribution is needed, but it cannot be seen as an exclusive contribution. The students bring their own experiences to contribute, and as we share our contributions, their wisdom and perspectives must be respected, valued, and explored.

Knowing this shifts the purpose of my relationship with my students from just teaching content, teaching to the test, teaching for a grade, to teaching and learning with my students in order to intentionally inspire, affirm, guide, collaborate, and celebrate each step in our process of becoming our very best selves. If the purpose of school, the purpose of our classrooms, is going to be to unlock and empower a passion for learning, we must develop and embrace a mindset that affirms cooperative, intergenerational relationships. In reading this book, I am excited for you to now join the Purpose-Driven Learning community of educators. Let us proudly share with our students and their families, our colleagues and administrators, our vision for a new story of learning. It will be an epic narrative that our students will write, share, and cherish long after their time in our school – a Purpose-Driven story of authentic, holistic, lifelong learning.